It's about... YO-CCK-030

**PUZZLEZ AND STORIEZ AND
GAMEZ FOR BRAINZ!**

THE WORLD'S BESTSELLING

ZOMBIES FOR Zombies

THE PLAY & WERK BUK

WITHDRAWN

Internal Images: © Lisa F. Young/dreamstime.com; © Xicoputini/dreamstime.com; © Simone Manzoni/dreamstime.com; © Catalin Petolea/dreamstime.com; © Helen Panphilova/dreamstime.com; © Louis Capeloto/dreamstime.com; © Vinicius Tupinamba/dreamstime.com; © Cynthia Farmer/dreamstime.com; © Grecu Mihail Alin/dreamstime.com; © Daniel Burch/Fotolia.com; © Silvia Bogdanski/Fotolia.com; © Vinicius Tupinamba/Fotolia.com; © Bondarau/Fotolia.com; © Art_man/Fotolia.com; © Tomasz Trojanowski/Fotolia.com; © Marcel Mooij/Fotolia.com; connor_robinson/iStockphoto.com; cynoclub/iStockphoto.com; DOUGBERRY/iStockphoto.com; panchof/iStockphoto.com; sjlocke/iStockphoto.com
Sourcebooks and the colophon are registered trademarks of Sourcebooks, Inc.

Published by Sourcebooks, Inc.
P.O. Box 4410, Naperville, Illinois 60567-4410
(630) 961-3900
Fax: (630) 961-2168
www.sourcebooks.com

Library of Congress Cataloging-in-Publication Data
Murphy, David P.
   Zombies for zombies : the play and werk buk : the world's bestselling inactivity guide for the living dead / by your host David P. Murphy ; illustrations by Daniel Heard.
      p. cm.
1. Zombies—Humor. I. Heard, Daniel, ill. II. Title.
   PN6231.Z65M876 2009
   814'.6–dc22

                              2010032547

                    Printed and bound in Canada.
                    WC 10 9 8 7 6 5 4 3 2 1

Contents

WHAT TO READ

WHAT YOU SENT US

ACKKKKNOWLEDGMENTS

To my family, immediate and extended, for your belief and support.

And especially to Dylan, who's one of the strongest humans I know; he makes Hercules look like a colossal weenie.

Daniel Heard: thanks again for a remarkably sick effort.

Laurie Fox: grande gratitude in your direction along with a sincere wish that the world will soon get to see more of *your* writing. Oh, and let's get on with that musical!

Thanks once more to Linda and Gary at the Linda Chester Literary Agency.

Peter Lynch: Yet again, you made everything easy. My sincere thanks. I sure am glad you're as bent as I am.

And to everyone else at Sourcebooks who was involved with this book in any way, thank you.

To all my friends in Omaha, Los Angeles, the Bay Area, Hastings, and elsewhere—I'm lucky to know you all.

And lastly, to the post-lifers, Horde members, and zombies, you had me at "Ackkkfff." Love and gizzards, Murphy

Life is pleasant. Death is peaceful.
It's the transition that's troublesome.

—Isaac Asimov

Enjoy yourself. It's later than you think.

—Chinese Proverb

A FOREWORD BY YOUR PRESIDENT,

President Dutch Bingo

(Brought to you, in part, by a grant from
The QualiCorps Foundation –
"Your friend in the future.")

My fellow Americans:

This last decade has been demanding, to say the least. Between the emergence of the P1V1 Virus, the resulting Disaster, and the economic struggles we've faced defending our nation, I don't need to tell you the toll it's taken on me. Truth is, what's left of my hair has now turned completely gray and, understandably, I'm totally freaking about that.

As you know, in order to survive as a country, it was necessary to make cutbacks and difficult choices. One of the toughest choices was to downsize our states from 50 to 37, a move for which I continue to take a large amount of shit. Do you think I *wanted* to do that? Besides, how often did we even *use* North Dakota?

My friends, we're in debt up to our collective nards for a number of reasons, but mostly because we're still having to build Containment Zones like crazy and those suckers don't come cheap. In addition, the Horde continues to escape and find pricey ways to retaliate against us, like blowing up gas stations or malls. With the most recent attack, I'm now faced with a situation where the nearest Spencer's store is now *over an hour away*. When will the heartache end?

Without the extraordinary generosity and corporate kwan of The QualiCorps Foundation, along with the additional capital generated by the National 24/7 Konstant Keno Kontest, we'd be in even deeper fiscal doodoo and couldn't afford the recently enacted Scarlet Shores Expansion Act, which is a humdinger piece of legislation, if I do say so myself. For their bigheartedness, I would encourage you to show your gratitude to QualiCorps as frequently as your wallets allow.

Make no mistake—we *will* survive. If I learned anything from my years as a voiceover artist, it was this: perseverance will take you farther than nepotism. I must admit that such a doggedly disciplined approach was never my strong suit but, I guarantee you, I'm continuing to act like I'm working on it.

On a side note, I understand many of you consider me to be shallow and cowardly but, may I remind you, I didn't ask for this job. I was perfectly *happy* being your Vice-President. For the record, I still feel very badly that I was probably partially responsible for getting our former President infected. What can I say—that Horde member was wearing a very convincing costume.

Today I will sign into law the National Renaming Act, whereby our beloved country can now alternately and legally be referred to as "Amer-I-CAN." By adopting this feel-good moniker, we'll be able to reinforce everything noble about this place, creating one hellacious warm and fuzzy feeling. This new law will, of course, simultaneously offer us possibilities for further corporate sponsorships. I'm aware there are certain citizens who'd like to be "all up in my grill" about pandering to the global conglomerates, but we *must* move forward with vision, optimism, and as many endorsements as we can nail. Holy cannoli, people—did I mention we need the cash?

Speaking of endorsements, I recently stumbled upon Mr. Murphy's fanciful tome, *The Play & Werk Buk*. I found it inspiring and Daniel Heard's drawings to be a wonder. I heartily recommend it for the living and post-living alike. If you *have* been recently bitten, it's your patriotic duty to force yourself to read this book so that you can remain a valued member of our citizenry. If you have *not yet* been bitten, then simply enjoy this book for the frivolous piece it is, while waiting for the worst to happen.

As always, I ask you to remain diligent (*not* the character in this book) in helping us keep the Horde in check. If you see a free-ranger, you are *urged* to pick up a National White Courtesy Phone and immediately report your sighting to the Paraguard. Such conscientiousness will, in the end, help to preserve our standard of living (if you can still call it that without laughing).

Enjoy *The Buk* and what's left of your days. May God bless.

Yours,

Your President,
President Dutch Bingo

INTRODUCTION

Hello, my name's David P. Murphy. Perhaps you remember me as the author of the world-famous *Zombies for Zombies: Advice and Etiquette for the Living Dead.* Or maybe you've seen me on television, pitching the entire line of *Sluggie* products, the world's first wearable blanket to feature Pharmaphibre™ technology.

If you know me, then you know that "integrity" is more than just a word to me—it's a way of life. I wouldn't be doing those *Sluggie* ads or hosting the Internet game show *Name That Bra Size! and* Fox's *Are You Dumber Than a Bag of Hammers?* if I didn't believe in what I do.

GREAT, ANOTHER SELF-PROMOTING TWIT.

No—hear me out. I come to you today because, honestly, I must get a request or two every few months for a companion guide to *Zombies for Zombies*. My office floor is littered with fan mail, ladies' underwear, and notes from folks whose lives were dramatically improved by the *Z4Z* program. Think I'm fibbing? Hey, I'm used to that. Check out these random excerpts:

- ⊙ "I don't know where I'd be today if not for your book. Actually, I do—probably in a Containment Zone!"— *Daryl B., Ottumwa, IA*
- ⊙ "With those dynamic diction lessons, I can now be understood some of the time!"—*Sarah L., Palmcaster, CA*
- ⊙ "Loved the visual tests and games. I think you should do an entire book of little things like that. There, I said it. Now, can I *please* get back that eighty bucks I loaned you?"—*My cousin Frank, knocking on my front door*

Frank, thanks for that last note (and the check IS in the mail).

After reading everyone's suggestions about what I should do with my next book (some of which can*not* be shared here), my focus group and I were finally able to drill down on the one section of *Z4Z* that was the most popular—the first chapter. (It was so popular, I hear, because that's as far as many of my readers got.) Chapter One was the part of *Z4Z* that contained, among other things, a quiz, a "which of these are not the same" game, and the whimsical diction lessons. Folks wrote in to tell me those particular exercises were extremely beneficial to their long-term recovery. They also said the games provided a heapin' helpin' of much-needed levity to individuals in the throes of the Transition (the approximate 72-hour state between life and post-life that occurs as a result of being infected by the Provo Virus).

The aforementioned focus groups discovered another strong component of that first chapter: more pictures and fewer words. Apparently, the later chapters with *fewer* pictures and *more* words left some readers in the dust and, I must tell you, I feel bad about that. Rest assured, I won't make the same mistake twice.

So, in response to the demand for a companion piece, I offer you *Zombies for Zombies: The Play & Werk Buk*.

The thing is, up to now, *The Buk* was only available to the post-life consumers residing at the Scarlet Shores chain of assisted post-living facilities. Based on its popularity there, I was asked to create a slightly different version of *The Buk* that might be accessible to the rest of the world, too—a hybrid for humans *and* post-lifers alike. Who was I to argue with such a request and possible money-maker?

Sure, you homo sapiens might find *The Buk* simplistic at times. But I think that after you read it, you *will* experience results eerily similar to those of the post-life contingent—a noticeable boost in brainpower and increased clarity in your thinky processes. The esteemed Dr. Kenneth Beaker, honored for his work with the post-living, has described *The Buk* as "a roto-rooter for the neural netways…you'd have to be a complete imbecile to NOT get *something* out of this." Thanks for the shout-out, Kenny!

Inside *The Play & Werk Buk*, you'll discover amusing new methods to help you maximize your QScale number (the sophisticated system by which we *all* can quantify our level of intelligence) *and* minimize your capacity to groan. Even if, as a soon-to-be post-lifer, you never read the first *Z4Z* (poor bastard), this Buk will delight and challenge you as you wait for your CareBox to arrive (which naturally includes a generous selection of powerful drugs and other helpful items).

WHO ELSE DO YOU HAVE WITH YOU? EW, IS THAT A CLOWN?

But forgive me, I've been rude and haven't introduced the rest of the cast from *Z4Z*. Let's take a moment to get reacquainted with our returning *dramatis personae* (and their new "Li'l" versions, too) along with a bitchin' pair of newbies. These charming characters will serve as your co-hosts at various points throughout:

This upstanding citizen is "Diligent," the good guy in the *Z4Z* world. Prior to being bitten, he was a word-processing operator for a major law firm, which gave him the emotional stamina to deal with post-life issues. If he looks familiar to you, it's because, since arriving on the post-life scene, Diligent has risen from simple "bitee" to semi-celebrity status, i.e. "playuh."

Here's "Doris," the chanteuse of our group. Doris is known for her effervescent personality and her seemingly limitless enthusiasm. It's infectious, isn't it? You may also recognize her from her appearances as a Shores Shopping Network Sales Hostess. Her bubbly personality, is what first caught Diligent's working eye and the two of them have been a mostly on-again couple for the last several months. In Doris' spare time (which is considerable), she enjoys reality shows, cotto salami, staring into space, and copious amounts of liquor.

Doofus is, quite simply, a bad egg. Just look at him—nothing good will happen with him around. He's our token member of the Horde (or he could be called a "zombie" if you prefer the old-fashioned vernacular). He was the "person" responsible for biting Diligent. Doofus is a trickster and will pose as anything from a doctor to a mystic. Don't listen to him or let him lure you into less-than-ideal situations. Beware the Doof!

Perhaps our most important character of all: Your Brain. This unfortunate creature never quite got the appropriate props from its appearances in Z4Z. Consequently, we're gonna make an effort to really show it the love this time. In the meantime, what YOU can do to help Your Brain's cause is to give *The Buk* your best shot. All the ginko biloba in Machu Picchu ain't gonna do jack squat if you don't push the envelope a bit harder, Chuck. Your Brain needs you and, need I say, you need it.

I am pleased to introduce two new characters:

This frightening fool is Chomps the Clown. A regular clown is creepy enough, but a living dead clown? It's a whole bowl of wrong. Children cry just at the sound of his name. Chomps' publicity agent would have you believe he's well meaning, yet his job as a corporate heavy tends to contradict this notion. Nota bene: if you ever see him in person, don't ask him about the New York Jets. Better yet, don't ask him anything—questions make him angry.

No Play & Werk Buk would be complete without a unicorn. Sadly, ours got infected by a dead polo player months ago. Now he's known as Horny, the Living Dead Unicorn, and he's the perkiest decomposing mythical animal ever. Plus, he's our country's number-one motivational speaker. Horny looks forward to moseying along with you on your journey through this Buk. Do yourself a favor, though: when he asks you for sugar cubes, which he inevitably will, don't get your hands anywhere near his mouth—just throw him the cubes.

My first book began: "So you've been bitten by a zombie? Bummer."

Well, the *bummer* just got *funner*!

YEAH, WELL, JUST KEEP THAT CLOWN AWAY FROM ME.

No problem.

As you frolic through this frisky inactivity guide, you'll have the time of your life (or upcoming post-life) with features such as:

- "The Recent Adventures of Li'l Doofus and Diligent"
- The continuing antics of "The Dead Bear Family"
- "Jamble"—that pain-in-the-ass scrambled word game
- Werd Surches and Crozzwerdz Gamez, some of which were designed by Phil Shortz, the opportunistic estranged younger brother of the respected puzzler!
- Thinky Thingz That Could Make Yer Hed Herty
- The Page YOU Made
- Solid advice from "Ask The Screaming Man"
- A coloring placemat/menu from Cap'n Ash's Seafood Fortress
- Two pages of paper dolls. 'Nuff said!
- Four brand-new, already beloved episodes of "Scarlet Storiez"

For those in the Transition, think of *The Buk* like this: Better to kill time than humans!

Right now, I can hear a few readers out there making comments such as "Does this book *ever* start?" or "Why is such a Buk even necessary?" Here's my response: "necessary" is an ugly word—like "should," but with more letters. As the saying goes, "All work and no play makes Jack a dead boy." I, for one, believe that this Jack person deserves more than a life of being dead.

WHATEVER. CAN I START PLAYING IN *THE BUK* NOW?

In a moment, but first I need you to understand that post-life isn't all about fun and play. For the recently bitten, there's a positive health benefit to werking this Buk. In fact, independent studies have found that those who complete the "enhanced program" (*both Z4Z* books) may experience a significant boost in the quality of their post-life. Additionally, those same individuals stand a twenty-two percent better chance of getting placed in a Scarlet Shores facility. These numbers may not mean much to you now, but could become increasingly important in your near future.

As you progress through *The Play & Werk Buk*, you'll most likely notice that the games and puzzles are of varying difficulty levels; some are challenging, some are themselves somewhat "challenged." Don't get discouraged. In designing this Buk, I worked closely with mental health professionals, cognitive specialists, and David Caruso in order to get the proper balance of stimulating *and* vapid. What this means is that you'll occasionally find certain brain-busters have been simplified, with you in mind. As the always insightful Doris says, "What good is a puzzle if you can't solve it?"

As your host, I wish you a wonderful romp through *The Buk*. And please don't blame our talented illustrator for "The Page YOU Made"—it's entirely my fault (and, of course, *yours*).

Game on!

David P. Murphy,
Maui Fortress #12

ZOMBIES FOR Zombies
THE PLAY & WERK BUK

So here's where I hand the steering wheel over to my trusted colleague, Diligent. He'll be chauffeuring you through the bulk of *The Buk*.

Diligent is one heck of a guy and the most genuine person I know. Don't think for a moment that you're being left in the care of a sickly stranger; it's not like that at all.

Hey, pally—howzabout you take it from here?

Sure thing, Dave. Welcome. I'm Diligent and, as Dave said, my friends and I will serve as your guides. Are you ready to be challenged? Are you still capable of using a pencil without injuring yourself? Are you even listening? Okay, good! Let's get this rolling!

Everyone loves a Werd Surch puzzle. Am I right or what?

WERD SURCH 1

Answers on page 99.

```
S  P  L  E  E  N  H  E
B  K  A  R  M  Z  E  C
R  N  U  T  Z  L  R  H
O  E  G  L  G  Y  N  E
M  E  R  U  L  S  I  N
E  C  R  N  E  W  A  E
R  A  R  G  G  H  Z  Y
I  P  R  G  Z  O  C  L
N  G  O  N  E  R  R  O
Q  U  L  A  J  D  U  R
C  H  E  W  Y  E  N  G
M  M  M  M  O  Z  C  A
L  I  F  E  R  R  H  N
P  I  V  O  T  A  G  Z
L  A  C  K  F  F  R  K
Q  U  A  L  I  K  O  E
```

Can YOU find these hidden werdz?

SKULL	ARGGH	CHEWY	ORGANZ
SIN	NUTZ	GLEE	ZED
ARMZ	KNEECAP	QUALIKO	LUNG
HERNIA	GRRRR	GNAW	SPLEEN
LIFER	LEGZ	RARE	CHENEY
HORDE	GONER	ACKFF	CRUNCH
PIVOT	MMMM	GROWL	ROMERIN

(Remember to check the diagonals, too—some may even be backwards!)

The Recent Adventures Of
LI'L DOOFUS AND DILIGENT

TODAY'S EPISODE: BLACK FRIDAY!!

Doofus behaves badly at the shopping mall.

Diligent resists the bad urges and eats at the food court.

Doofus shoves aside waiting customers to get into the dressing room first.

Diligent allows others to use the dressing room before him.

Doofus exhibits a lack of self-control in the pet store.

Diligent and Doris admire the baby bunnies.

Since Diligent's still moistening bunnies on the prior page, I'll fill in for a sec.

Remember me? Hope so, because I'm Your Brain. Here's a favorite game of mine/yours. Circle the next best sequential word in the list below to keep your QScale number rising.

Answers on page 99.

Alllllllll aboard—

THE QSCALE EXPRESS!

1. bad, bead, bled, —
    a. boo-tay
    b. beef
    c. boink
    d. bleed

2. fave, fever, save, —
    a. favre
    b. severe
    c. flave
    d. sever

3. gnash, gnaw, nosh, —
    a. now
    b. owwee
    c. gosselin
    d. gash

4. flim, flam, limb, —
    a. flan
    b. loogie
    c. lamb
    d. yum

5. ran, rein, van, —
    a. vanna
    b. vein
    c. velour
    d. sajak

6. bill, bound, will, —
    a. smith
    b. wanna
    c. wound
    d. wonka

7. mold, mood, fold, —
    a. farkle
    b. fudd
    c. feud
    d. food

8. brat, bread, hat, —
    a. hatter
    b. hattest
    c. hert
    d. head

9. hag, hug, drag, —
    a. droog
    b. queen
    c. prey
    d. drug

10. alter, falter, ire, —
    a. uhhhhhhhhh
    b. die?
    c. fire
    d. fester

CROZZWERDZ 1

Holy crap! Are ya tryin' to hurt me here?!

All the werdz below still have their Zs. Your mission is to move left to right and down, filling in the werdz below, using the unnumbered cluez. The numberz in parenz next to the cluez represent the number of letterz in that werd. Got a headache yet?

Answers on page 99.

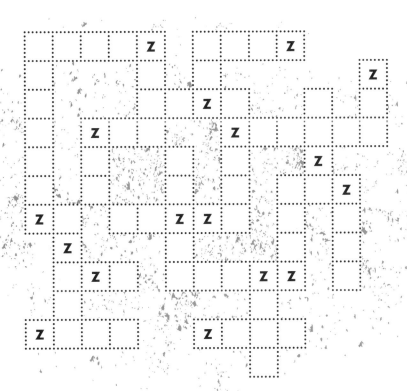

ACROSS

Dumb blue jewel (5)

Jewish dork (4)

"Don't ____ me, bro" (4)

Not very delicious primitive life form (3)

Past tense nothing, nada, squat (6)

"Oh yeah? ___ you!" (3)

Abbreviation of Dutch Zuid-Afrika (2)

DJ _____ Jeff or Fosse-esque (5)

Evil gun that will do no good (3)

Creepy substance forming on your skin (5)

What you'll probably lack soon or a brand of soap (4)

Containment? (4)

DOWN

German for "proclivity for" (sounds like "bands of connective tissue") (7)

Sixth letter of dumb Greek alphabet (4)

A candy whose dispenser head comes off (3)

Nickname for zombie (3)

Online auction site for dummeez (5)

To catch some zzzzzzzs (4)

Gated community for yummy critters (3)

Synonym for nimrods or brand of clowns (5)

Some dumb canal (4)

Some dumb mineral (4)

Even dumber shade of blue (5)

A type of funny that never is (4)

SHUFFLECRAFT SAFETY INACTIVITY PAGES

Cpl. Lance Doofus of the Paraguard and part-time driver for the ShuffleCraft Force, says:

Listen up, mateys: your safety is my primary concern. Ackkkkffff!

Sooner than you think, you *could* be dependent on the ShuffleCraft system for your transportation needs. This is because, if you're old enough to drive, that privilege is soon going away. However, worry not— our sleek fleet of ShuffleCrafts is ready to serve you 19/6! Check out this page for vital info.

There are only a handful of simple rules to know when riding the Crafts. Adhere to these and no one gets hurt:

- ⊙ Always check the schedule so that you won't be mistaken for a bum or detained as a loiterer.
- ⊙ Stand away from the curb because the driver could be texting.
- ⊙ Or watching sitcoms on his phone.
- ⊙ They do enjoy their mobile sports programs, too.
- ⊙ Remember, when making the rounds, the Crafts don't really *stop*, per se. Your recommended approach when boarding: as the Craft rolls by, tightly grab the guardrails and hop on.
- ⊙ No shoving or grunting allowed.
- ⊙ Once seated, stay put. Don't *even* think about getting up until the Craft reaches your destination.
- ⊙ Don't screw around with the Happy Harness.
- ⊙ The Crafts are non-non-smoking zones; smoke 'em if you've got 'em.
- ⊙ Keep your arm inside the vehicle.
- ⊙ Do not speak to the Ground Marshal.
- ⊙ Obey the driver or suffer stamp penalties.
- ⊙ Never bite the Craft or, need we say, any fellow commuters.
- ⊙ Clean up your own drool.
- ⊙ When exiting the Craft, a running jump is recommended.

SHUFFLECRAFT SHUFFLEFACTS!

- ⊙ The average Craft moves at a manageable 4 miles per hour.
- ⊙ The ShuffleCraft safety record was spotless until the last 3 years.
- ⊙ The fleet was designed by a distant cousin of the visionary who created the Ford Fiesta.
- ⊙ ShuffleCraft Drivers are tested annually to ensure that their skill sets are in keeping with industry substandards.
- ⊙ No ShuffleCrafts run on Sundays and they are <u>**not**</u> in service any day between 1 and 6 a.m.
- ⊙ Your President, President Dutch Bingo, likes the ShuffleCrafts so much that he got one of his own to toodle around in within his compound.

COLOR ME "MOBILE!"

Whip out your crayons and have at it!

☛SHAPE☛ UP✐!

Logic games aren't just for those nerdy Vulcans anymore; you'll enjoy this, too.

And when you're done, see what your score tells you about YOU.

And remember that these particular problems get more difficult as you progress.

Matter of fact, the last few are plain icky.

Answers and Score Key on page 100.

1. ☐ - ■ - ▣ - ?

   a.  ◈

   b. ⬤

   c.  👂

   d. ▫

2.  ◀◀ - ▶▶ - ▌◀◀ - ?

   a. 🐈

   b. 🐕

   c. 🐦

   d. ▶▶▌

3.  ☉ - ◉ - ○ - ?

   a.  👽

   b. ↺

   c. ●

   d.  🚭

4.  ✡ - ☪ - ☯ - ?

   a. 💰

   b.  ☎

   c.  ೞ

   d. ✝

Jeepers, enough already!
This stuff is taxing!

5. ↖ - ↗ - ↙ - ?

   a. ♫

   b. 👄

   c. 🌍

   d. ↘

6. ☺ - ☹ - ✳ - ?

   a. 💣

   b. ✴

   c. ☑

   d. ☠

7. ↓↑ - 🚲 - ✈ - ?

   a. 👁

   b. ≋

   c. ♉

   d. ↯

8. ß - Ç - Þ - ?

   a. wtf

   b. 😐

   c. ‽

   d. µ

TREAZURE HUNT!

The Li'ls have taken a field trip to the QCasino to look for the sorta-hidden objects. Help the kidz find the items listed below!

LEG	TROWEL	CUP OF QUALICOLA	ROSE
BOTTLE OF PILLS	PUDDLE OF DROOL	TOOTH	CHAIN SAW
RIFLE	KITTEN	BOMB	COLORADO

THINKY THINGZ THAT COULD MAKE YER HED HERTY

Can you answer these without hemorrhaging?

How many consonants are you still able to name?

Name three places where you can obtain meat.

How many words can you think of that mean the same thing as "ow"?

Take your index finger and try to touch your nose. How much of it is still there?

Can you explain why questions end in a question mark? Okay smarty, then why isn't a period called a "statement mark"?

What's the difference between a duck?

In the drawing below, why is a dog in the aquarium?

NOW how many consonants can you name?

"There," "their," "they're." What the heck?

If you were an Osmond Brother, which one would you be? Which one would your mom be? And your dad? Why is no one ever "Merrill"?

Jamal has four nickels and a liquor stamp. What can he do with that?

If I told you Glenn Beck's middle name is "Hussein," what would you think?

Not to harp, but how's that consonant issue comin' along for ya?

Can you remember the last name of your first kill? How about the first of your last?

What percentage of Harry Reid's body has been replaced by bionics?

Gramma used to say, "Keep the hell off my lawn, Jimmy." What did she mean?

Why might men want to wear pants in public?

A typical human has how many teeth? And you?

"Goose" is to "foie gras" as "screaming white girl in a graveyard" is to _____?

"Eve of Destruction" — yes or no?

SALLY'S *BIG* ADVENTURE

Sally had moved into her house just nine days ago. It was a pretty yellow house with sky-blue trim and a lovely wooden fence surrounding it. Sally didn't know Omaha very well yet, especially her neighborhood. "Little Italy" they called it; it was next to another area Sally's parents called "Little Appalachia." Her parents always laughed when they said that, so Sally did too.

Omaha sure is a lot different than Hastings, Nebraska, Sally thought. In her former hometown, she could ride her bike all day and visit anywhere she liked. In Omaha, however, she'd already been warned several times by her mom and dad not to travel too far, not to stay out past dusk, not to talk to their Negro neighbors, and that she should absolutely not ride her bike anywhere close to the enormous boat-like structure down by the Missouri River, a half-mile away. It even had a name: Scarlet Shores Beta. Sally thought this sounded exotic; she could even see the faux crow's-nest top of the structure from her bedroom window. She imagined that if she ever somehow got into that crow's nest, the view would be incredible.

All the talk and warnings about the place made Sally even more curious. And so, several days later, Sally decided it was time to go on a journey to check out this mysterious place and, like that bear that went over that mountain, to see what she could see.

The evening before her adventure, Sally was talking with her new friend Rosa, a bubbly little Hispanic girl who was one year younger than Sally. When Sally brought up Scarlet Shores, Rosa's eyes grew wide and whispered several words under her breath that must've been in Spanish because they made no sense to Sally. Then Rosa proceeded to tell Sally everything she knew about the place: no one was allowed to go near it; there were bad people in there who'd caught bad colds and they'd like to give you a cold, too; monsters lived on the other side of that fence and they'd love to escape and blow up a mall or move into your closet; and that even though the place looked fun from the outside, it wasn't. It had cooties—*big* cooties. Rosa yammered on and on and Sally eventually tuned her out, dreaming of dinner and candy.

The next afternoon, Sally told her mom she was going down the street to visit Rosa but, instead, she pedaled like mad, up and down the hills of Little Italy, heading in the direction of that crow's nest. Finally, she crossed the railroad tracks, right where the old levee was. Sally had never had an adventure this big before and was mighty excited. Coming to a stop, she took a breath and looked up. Immediately before her was the large structure she'd been warned about, sitting on the edge of the blue-brown waters of the Missouri.

It doesn't look so scary, Sally thought. The place was shimmering and ultra-white, and gave off an aroma of fresh bread and chlorine.

Sally ditched her bike in the nearby brush and made her way toward the shiny building. She moved slowly and quietly, because she could see a number of people standing around on the other side of the tall, tall chain-link fence and she didn't want them to notice her.

Sally crouched behind a bush, then peeked around it to watch what was going on. She spotted about eight or nine strangely dressed people moving around in a silly manner—sort of how Daddy walked when he came home late from work. She couldn't be sure about what these people were doing. It looked like they were performing an odd dance but there wasn't any music playing. Not only that, the people were stepping forward in a deliberate way and stood far apart, not talking to one another.

Over on the far side of what Sally now assumed to be a vast, plush front yard, she saw two men dressed up in important-looking uniforms, like the policemen who visited her school or those loud men at her uncle's rally who dressed all in brown. The uniformed men appeared to be playing a card game and were paying no attention to the slow-dancing folks.

Just as she was trying to peer over the bush a bit more aggressively, a gnat flew up her nose. Shoot, Sally thought, I'm gonna sneeze!

She tried to cover her mouth and nose, but wasn't quick enough. The bug tickled the inside of her nose and, sure enough, a semi-muffled, high-pitched sneeze came shooting out of her. Sally immediately crouched back down, attempting to hide in the bush. "Oh no," Sally whispered. One of those dancing people appeared to have heard her and turned his head. And to make things worse, he began to stumble toward her.

Gritting her teeth, Sally sat motionless and decided that if she closed her eyes, the dancing man might go away. (Sometimes Sally lived in denial.) Now she heard leaves rustle, followed by a grunt. She opened her eyes and gasped. There, just a few feet from her, was the unusual-looking man staring at her through the fence and smiling. He said something to her that she couldn't understand and made a gesture that looked friendly. He seems like a nice fellow, thought Sally approvingly.

She slowly emerged from behind the bush and cautiously approached him. As she did, the man appeared to vibrate, as if he was really, really happy. She tried not to look at him too closely, because she was still thinking about what Rosa had said. She didn't want *anyone* moving into her closet, thank you very much.

"What's your name, mister?" Sally asked.

Sally received an answer that she couldn't figure out. She thought he said "Jiminy" but it could have been "Jeff."

She decided to compromise and asked, "Jiffy?"

He nodded.

"That's a nifty name!" she exclaimed and instantly decided that she liked him.

While Jiffy stared at her, Sally began to look at him a little closer. His clothes were funny—nothing seemed to really fit him. As she heard her mom say once, it looked like he got dressed in the dark.

The fellow reminded Sally of one of those peculiar guys she'd seen at the Comic Convention last year when her cousin forced her to go with him and the whole experience made her cry. Shaking off the memory, Sally refocused and muttered,

"Poor man, I'll cheer him up." She then spotted a nearby patch of wildflowers and skipped over it.

Upon finding the lone, perfect white flower in the patch, Sally picked it, turned, and carefully returned to the fence, still trying to make sure no one else saw her. She could tell that nobody was even aware that Jiffy was so close to her.

Extending the flower to him through the fence, Sally exclaimed, "Here Jiffy, this is for you."

Jiffy slowly crouched down, at which point Sally could hear his body creak and she could actually smell him! He needs Daddy's cologne, she thought.

Then she gave him an even closer look, and immediately her stomach felt weird. He had a face like a Halloween mask. While Sally was distracted by his curious features, she realized Jiffy was now holding her hand along with the flower. Just as she began to get scared, he looked into her eyes, smiled crookedly, put his lips to her hand and kissed it.

Sally giggled at the kiss. His lips felt like cold marmalade. Still smiling at her, he held the flower to his mostly missing nose and appeared to inhale its scent. Then he leaned in to kiss her hand again but, this time, he gave it a little nip as he let it go.

"Ow! Hey, Jiffy, that hurt and it wasn't nice at all," Sally whispered.

Jiffy kind of shrugged, smiled, flashed the flower at her and turned to walk away.

"Well, please don't do it again," she chastised him. After a moment, she brightened and asked, "I'll see you again sometime, right?"

Jiffy nodded as he continued to walk.

"Uh-oh," Sally said, as she noticed it was almost dusk. She realized she'd been gone too long. She ran back to where she'd stashed her bike, quickly hopped onto it, and pedaled like crazy. Climbing the hills, she coasted through the valleys. She hoped her mom wasn't getting worried or calling Rosa's house.

Sally wheeled into her own driveway as her mom was stepping out the front door. She was wearing that concerned look of hers and Sally felt bad. Sally explained she'd been playing on the computer with Rosa and had lost track of time. Her mom seemed to relax and gave her a big hug, telling Sally not to worry her again.

As they walked toward the house, Sally's mom asked, "What happened to your hand, honey? You've got a little cut."

Surprised to see a small amount of blood on her hand, Sally thought quickly and said, "I helped Rosa in the garden earlier."

"Let's wash that right now and get a Band-Aid on it."

The rest of the evening couldn't have been nicer. Sally's dad was walking normally and her mom was humming and chain-smoking in the kitchen. Sally kept thinking about Jiffy and how much she liked his twisted smile. Sure, she wished he hadn't accidentally bit her, but she thought he was still awful nice.

The next morning, Sally felt crummy when she woke up. Her mom confirmed that she had a low-grade fever and must have caught a bug (and, this time, not a gnat). Then her mom disappeared for a few minutes as Sally waited for better news. After a phone call to the school, her mom reentered Sally's bedroom and gave her an update: Sally was to stay home from school, have chicken soup, and sleep all day. Yippee, Sally thought, and sneezed the biggest sneeze she'd ever sneezed.

QUIZZZTIME!!!: SALLY'S BIG ADVENTURE

Please circle the correct answers.

Or cheat here: page 100.

1. Sally obeyed her parents.
   True   False

2. Sally's parents are bigots.
   True   False

3. Rosa was a Serb.
   True   False

4. Little girls are always welcome at Scarlet Shores Beta.
   True   False

5. Jiffy was a nice man.
   True   False

6. Sally's dad came home from work happy.
   True   False

7. Sally's mom smokes like a chimney.
   True   False

8. Sally caught a cold from Jiffy.
   True   False

From the makers of **HammerMe Pain Negotiator** comes the evolution of over-the-counter medication:

SLEDGE®

Sledge is the first HammerMe-related product that not only lessens your pain, but also contains an incredibly potent sleeping agent.

Fast-acting Sledge is recommended for those who would simply like to doze their way through the Transition without having to deal with any symptoms, not to mention squirrelly advice from corporate scientists or hack writers. Effects last up to 72 hours.

Take two Sledge and find a soft surface—immediately. Really. And we're not kidding when we say "fast-acting." Do not try to operate a forklift or even a fork while taking Sledge. Don't begin a meal either unless you want to drown in your dinner.

Caution: Using Sledge will greatly impair your ability to be placed in a Scarlet Shores Assisted Post-Living Facility and could lead to Horde. We're just sayin'.

You'll wake up refreshed and hungry as hell.

SLEDGE®

"You won't know what hit you!"

YOU COMPLETE ME!

The solution to the clue in the left-hand column will be a word that is contained within
the solution to each clue in the right-hand column (hence the name of the puzzle).
For example, the word "ant" might be used to complete the word "plant."
Make sense? No? Okay, in other words, each word in the right-hand column
(once you figure out what that is) in each section can be completed
by solving the clue on the left. Any better? Still no? Then skip it. Yeesh!

Answers on page 100.

1. A chewy appendage on either side of the head.

   Booty-shaped fruit

   They're shed by sad people

   Fraidy cat trait

   Sweet superlative suck-up

2. "Oh no, you di'in't. You're tellin' me you ___ that kidney?!"

   Do the deed or another word for "bloke"

   Use this to shred the cheese, please

   Eating surfaces or meant to be spun

   Ask a stupid question and Chomps might do this to you
   (bonus points for this one)

3. How you're looking or geeks know it hangs out with LAN.

   Snobbish graceful bird

   Fades in a big way

   British nincompoop

   They've got a reward out for you

4. You either ___ or you aren't.

   Not the brightest majestic female racing critter

   Pink in the middle

   Here, take mine—I've got plenty

   You've got a lotta blank _____

5. A bonding agent for sentences.

   Lend me a ___

   Blah

   Beaches have wayyy too much of this

   Nachos' large other half
   (careful: this one's tricky!)

Connect Zee Dotz!

Our li'l hosts are back and it looks like they've got company! (Hint: ★ = pick up your pencil.)

THE PAGE YOU MADE

Another great batch of submissions, lifers. Keep up the dead work!

Kitty I Bit

Rexella V. I., Age 41
Missourinois

The Bunny

I saw him by the roadside
floppy ears and all
I only wanted to hold him
and see how he tasted
but he got scared
and ran away
just like my sister did
and all those friends I had
oh well
these blue pills help a lot
and the green ones too
they help me to forget
the bunny

Jason R., Age 32
Kanslahoma

How Long

How long until we all learn
to love one another?
Hug a Horde member today.

Female Horde member 14899993
Nashville Containment Zone

Puppet I Bit

Jimmy L., Age 18
Maryland

These Make Me Glad

Liquor stamps
lost, bewildered teens
Monday's mystery stew
humans huddled in a basement
cartoons
blood sausage
memories of my rampage
arteries
bluebirds
these make me glad

Donna L., Age 27
California

We Will Rise

We will rise.
The Great Pushback will fail.
And you—you *all* will die.

Angela M., Age 19
CouncilTucky Containment Zone

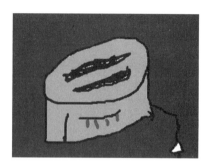

Toaster I Bit

Latravis R., Age 22
Vernhampshire

Why is it

i don't talk as well
as some of these other folks
maybe they started off smarter
to begin with
so they get to keep more of
their fancy-shmancy words
me, i sound like
"yyyyes, sssspuds and
ehhhh-extra meat sssstuff, too."
not exactly cool
but then again
i've got a fully recharged QCard
and three hot dates
this weekend.
in your face, former life!

Mark P., Age 47
Minnekota

Bird I Couldn't Get To

Biff M., Age 37
Utahdo

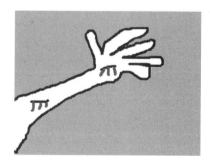

Arm I Bit (Twice!)

Ming X., Age 22
Florigia

Appearing this Sunday, from 1–2:30 p.m., at the Grand Reopening of the Pittsyldelphia Oakmont Park View Mt. St. Ruby's Quali-KoPlus...

This Nation's Favorite
Motivational Speaker

Horny,
THE LIVING DEAD UNICORN!

H-h-hey k-kidz—don't forget the s-s-sugar c-cubes!

Horny will be at QK+ to read selections from his heartwarming new book,

"THE END OF THE RAINBOW:
A Unicorn's Tail"

At the reading, find out how you and yours can get involved with
Horny's charitable foundation, *"KIDZ KOME FIRST"*!
Hear his stirring story.
Get your picture taken with him.
Have him stomp on your copy of the book.
Keep your hands the hell away from his mouth!

Horny will also be available afterwards, on a first-come first-served basis,
for private one-on-one counseling sessions.

*(Prices will be based on length of session and determined that day by Horny.
Sessions are subject to last-minute cancellation at the sole discretion of Horny.)*

I'll s-s-see you th-th-there!

THE DEADLY BLOCKS!

Take the letters in the word "MOO" and fill in the words beneath it. But remember:
you can only use each letter in "MOO" once in order to complete each row of
THE **DEADLY** BLOCKS!

Answers on page 100.

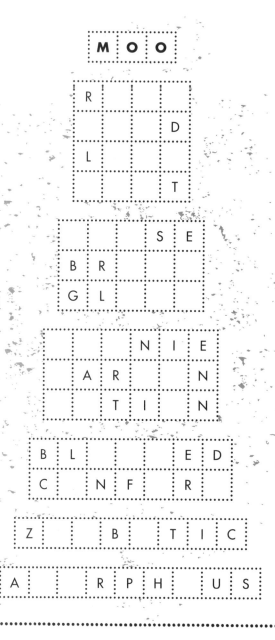

Take this page into **any** Cap'n Ash's restaurant and you'll get a free bag of six coloring markers* (and yes, at least three of them will be red). That way, while you're waiting for your order to arrive (some fish just don't die easily), you can while away the minutes "werking" on this page.

When I grow up (glug), I'm gonna be on the menu at Cap'n Ash's Seafood Fortress !! (glug)

Side Dishes:

#1 Chub Chowder
#2 Krill Dip 'n' Chips
#3 Slimehead Fries
#4 Potato Salad

Beverages:

QualiCola, Diet QualiCola, QualiCola Minus-2, Cherry QualiCola, QualiUP, & Ice Tea

Main Dishes:

#1 Sculpin Sticks
#2 Toothfish Tacos
#3 The "Pick Your Own"
   Lamprey Platter
#4 Crappie Po' Boy
#5 Gar Patty on a Bun

(Market prices on all menu items)

* Only one bag of markers per page, per customer. The Seafood Fortress is not responsible for what you do with the markers *after* they are given to you. Do not eat them, poke yourself with them, get them caught in your windpipe, insert them in your ears or, for that matter, your nose. As a rule of thumb (you remember thumbs), keep the markers away from *all* body cavities. They are only meant for coloring and they're free so, for Meep's sake, don't do something stupid like get a lawyer and file a claim if you hurt yourself. We'll destroy you in a courtroom.

HAVE YOU HAD YOUR P1V1 BOOSTER SHOT YET?

The P1V1 Booster Shot has gotten more than its share of negative, unfair publicity.

As a result, people are choosing to ignore the fact that the shot is necessary and required **BY LAW**.

Here are THE FACTS regarding the Booster Shot:

- There *was* an inferior batch of serum that got into the system two years ago. It caused a minute percentage of the populace to believe they were Argentinean tango dancers or were capable of communicating with wrens. Every batch since then has been fine. Really.
- Compounds that make up the shot are NOT derived from Horde urine.
- It is not possible to be allergic to the shot as its properties are almost entirely alien in nature.
- The shot will not help you if you've already entered the Transition. It is *only* for the uninfected. If you *have been* infected, report to your local P1V1 Conversion Center for assistance.
- No one has died from getting the shot.*
- There *are* no shortages of the vaccine, especially if you work for a Wall Street brokerage.
- For the men: no, it will *not* make (a) your erections last longer or (b) your wiener bigger. Please stop asking.
- The shot takes only a moment and is administered by a trained professional or an off-duty dietician.

So stop listening to the press and your stupid neighbor who doesn't know
what he's talking about. You know, the one who believes that a Chupacabra
is raiding his vegetable garden every night.

GET YOUR P1V1 BOOSTER SHOT TODAY!!

*Lately

HO HO HA HA HE HEEEEE ACKK ARGH ACKKFFFF!!!

YA GOTTA HAVE JÖKES!!!

Q: I'm normally used for gardening, but can frequently be found in a Horde member's forehead. What am I?
A: A trowel.

Maryann, Wisconsin

Innocent bystander: Uh, you're not gonna bite me, right?
Horde member: Of course not. Hey look, it's Halley's Comet!

Juan, Florigia

There was a post-lifer named Jiffy
who always dressed ever so spiffy.
But his teeth, I'm afraid
were gone or decayed
which made his smile even more iffy.

Herbie, S.S. Beta

Pen: I'm "inking" of a number between 1 and 10. What is it?
Paper: I don't know—6?
Pen: Damn it!

Princess Steve, Nevada

Q: What has thousands and thousands of heads, but not one working brain cell?
A: A Containment Zone!

Ezekiel, Montoming

Q: What's the difference between a lifer and a fern?
A: Not much.

Tony, Missourinois

Son: Mom, this darn studying makes me hungry!
Mom: Well, what are you reading?
Son: My biology textbook.

Admiral Winky, Utahdo

Knock knock.
Who's there?
Kenya.
Kenya who?
Kenya guess why I don't have a pulse?

Jack, Texarkansas

Q: How many Horde members does it take to screw in a light bulb?
A: Five—one to hold the bulb and the other four to ack argghh ackff.

Pablo, Newer Mexico

Innocent bystander: Uh, you're not thinkin' about tryin' to bite me, right?
Horde member: Why, never! Hey, check it out—when did the QualiKo Blimp get into town?

Biff, Connecticut

Post-lifer: What's up?
A fern: Not much. You?
Post-lifer: Not much. See ya.
A fern: Bye.

Tony, Missourinois

BRAIN LABYRINTH

That sentimental sap, Diligent, built Doris an elaborate brain-shaped hedge maze
for her birthday. Sure, it was a sweet gesture, but now he can't find his way
back through it and he isn't sure he built it correctly.
For the luvva Meep, find a path for him!

Answer on page 101.

Diligent says:

HEED THE CALL TODAY!

Carpe Mortius.

Seize the Dead!

Are you ready for the challenge of a lifetime?
Are you prepared to serve your country?
Then get ready to become a member of—

THE PARAGUARD

If you're still living, you'll most likely qualify for an exhilarating career with—

THE PARAGUARD

We're not like the other branches of the Armed Forces—our standards are far more reasonable, which means a greater chance for rapid advancement for you and your drop-out friends.

So quit listening to your stupid neighbors, the ones who think The Great Pushback will fail and the Horde will win. The Horde <u>will</u> be defeated and, so you know, your neighbors regularly huff Reddi-wip.

Come join us on the front lines of The Great Pushback and live out your vid-game dreams. We'll take away that candy-ass controller and give you a gun. Won't *that* be cool?!

This is **your** chance!

SEIZE THE DEAD!

JOIN

THE PARAGUARD

Contact us at 1-877-**PARAGEE**.

> Oh great, just because I'm the *girl*, I have to host a goofy crafts page? You boys are totally lame.

What a Load of Crafts!

We thought you might enjoy an old-school endeavor, one of those ancient, innocent inactivities your parents used to do on rainy afternoons before the rain became toxic. There's a certain simplistic pleasure to be found in this project so, of course, we thought of you!

Today, we're going to make a wounded human forearm/hand combo. This can be used for anything from biting practice to displaying it as a lovely *objet d'art*.

For this project we'll need (*see photo*):

- ⊙ Two (2) pieces of tan construction paper
- ⊙ Scissors (make sure you're cleared for scissor usage, which requires a Class 2 license or higher)
- ⊙ A sharpened pencil
- ⊙ Scotch tape
- ⊙ Glue
- ⊙ Elbow macaroni
- ⊙ A black crayon and a red crayon

(Note: consider keeping a few Band-Aids handy, just in case.)

1. Take the pencil and begin the project by placing your left hand (palm down) on a piece of construction paper. Trace around your hand as if you were going to make one of those kindergarten turkeys (you *know* what I'm talking about). While tracing, make sure to include part of your wrist because this will be where the "hand" attaches to the "forearm." When done, take your scissors (be careful, please) and cut out the paper silhouette of your hand. Dispose of the excess paper in an appropriate manner.

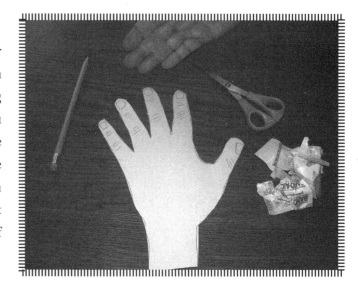

2. Lay the paper hand on the table and, using your pencil, draw fingernails and knuckles on the hand (*see photo*). In the project shown above, we created a male hand and arm. But you may choose to make it female and design your hand and arm accordingly (for example, use a red crayon to create colorful nail polish on nails). Whichever gender you choose, feel free to draw hair, warts, or whatever excites you.

3. Now, take the other piece of construction paper and roll it into a tube in a lengthwise manner. Using the tape, tape the overlapping edges in place so that the tube stays a tube once it's placed back on the table.

4. Picking up your pencil, be careful not to get overexuberant and stab yourself. Using a steady grip, sketch in, just as you did with the hand, whatever features you'd like your arm to have—hair, veins, a tattoo, etc. The photo below depicts the ever-popular "Mom" tattoo for this particular arm. You may also choose to use the black crayon to indicate darker features if you'd like.

5. Now, this is where it gets exciting. Grabbing the paper hand, gently insert the small "wrist" section into one end of the tube and place a piece of tape inside the tube, joining the tube and the paper hand together. Reinforce with additional pieces of tape as needed.

6. You should have a darn good-looking arm and hand by now. But it looks a little too *healthy*, wouldn't you agree?

7. Grab your black crayon and draw a straight line approximately 2–3 inches long on the outside part of the arm. Using your scissors again, carefully make a cut along the black line that you just drew. Warning: insert the point of the scissors *into the tube* and NOT *your own arm*.

8. Take your red crayon and, drawing downward from the cut on the arm, color in the blood that should be coming out of the cut. Size to taste.

9. Finally, because every craft project ever conceived finds a way to include glue and macaroni in the design, go ahead and do the same. Use the macaroni and glue to adorn the arm/hand with jewelry and rings if you'd like (*see photo*). If not, eat the glue and sniff the macaroni. Or is it the other way around?

10. Now admire your "hand"-iwork: a magnificent hand/arm combo to do with as you will!

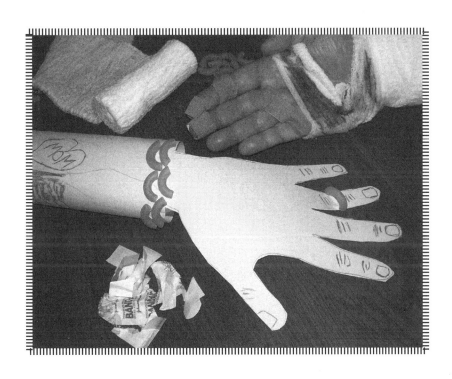

AND NOW, ANOTHER INSTALLMENT OF
"ASK THE SCREAMING MAN"

Wherein an anonymous mental health
professional with anger issues
answers your everyday questions
related to post-Disaster post-life and love.

Today's first query comes from a Mrs. Mabel Ridge in Shreveport, LA. She writes:

Dear Screaming Man: It seems that my husband has contracted some sort of vicious flu that's given him a powerful fever and appears to be causing a form of necrosis, otherwise known as skin decay. Could you please tell me what this might be? Our family physician seems baffled and my neighbors are stumped, too. My hubby Rodney's very sick and yet, he seems to perk up whenever he's served red meat. Thank you in advance for your assistance.

Dear Mabel: Maybe you haven't watched the TV or listened to the radio for the last, ohhhh say, nine years, but there's been this global pandemic thing going on that's making the dead rise. Is that ringing a bell for ya? I repeat, making the dead RISE. I mean, it's been sort of a BIG DEAL!! And you're telling me that your doctor and NONE of your friends or neighbors know *anything* about this? What the hell? I can't even *believe* you spent the time writing *me* when you should've been contacting the proper authorities and sealing off Rodney in a spare bedroom!! How much dumber can people g-g-g-GAGHHHHHHHHHHHH!!

Next up, Mr. Leroy Potts from Scarlet Shores Sacracisco has a personal issue:

Dear Screaming Man: I've only been at this facility for two days, but I'm already confused. The attendants tell me I'm not going to get better and that this is my new home. Well, I'll admit I'm currently not in tip-top shape, with the nasty shakes and crazy skin tone, but, come on, I don't belong here. The other residents are obviously sicker than I, and they appear to be in what I can only describe as a medicinal haze. Worst of all, everyone keeps trying to hit on me. Yuck. I've got to admit, I'm a little uncomfortable with this. What can you tell me?

Dear Leroy: Holy crap! Does anyone *ever* write a question to me that's *not* insane? Listen to me, Leroy: You've somehow contracted the Provo Virus. Because of this, you've been permanently relocated to the Scarlet Shores facility nearest to your home and you live *there* now! Did you NOT read *Zombies for Zombies*? If you didn't, how in the world did you even end up at a Scarlet Shores?

You need to start taking the recommended medicines immediately and make all the friends you can. You have NO IDEA how lucky you are. How can you people keep missing the point so b-b-b-BAUGHHHHHHHHHHHHHHHHHHHH!!!

And finally, Lt. Jerry Farner, who's stationed outside the Tempe Containment Zone, writes:

Dear Screaming Man: I'm currently in week nine of patrolling the lower quadrant of the C.Z. as part of The Great Pushback. Lately, it's been quiet—a "ranger" every now and then; that keep things interesting. When rangers do show up, we either ice 'em or tranq 'em and turn 'em over to our superiors. But here's what I don't get about this Zone: who's getting contained? Is it illegal aliens or are there "other" aliens in there? Guess I may have missed that part of the briefing that one day when I nodded out. Okay, man—later.

Dear Jerry: Why do I keep this lame job? It's not like I need the stamps. Month after month I deal with this *same* level of cluelessness. Here's what amazes me in your case, Jerry—they let *you* use a gun! While we're at it, why don't we put your dumb fingers on the BIG RED BUTTON, TOO?!! Mary, Mother of—Jerry, the *Horde* is being contained in there, okay? They're like the free-rangers you mentioned but many times worse. They're the ENEMY, Jer! We're pushing back against THEM and that's why you're patrolling the place. God help us, you're *supposedly* protecting us from them. Is it coming together for ya yet, Bucko? The Horde is a lot like zombies because they *are* zombies! That's why they're being *contained*, Jerry. And, that's why the word "containment" is in the term "Containment Z-Z-Z-ZARGHHHHHHHHHHHHH!!!"

Please join us again next time when The Screaming Man answers
your everyday questions related to post-Disaster post-life and love.
You can contact The Screaming Man at: screamingman@thescreamingman.com.

DED LIBZ!

Uhhhhhh, I don't get it.

Well, Doofus, that's okay because these Ded Libz aren't meant for you, anyway. Readers, I bet *you're* familiar with the drill: plug the numbered words from each of the first two columns into the appropriate blanks in the paragraph below and see how silly the story becomes. In the third column, create your own Ded Lib!

A LETTER HOME

Dear ___(1)___ and ___(2)___:

I'm finally starting to settle in here at ___(3)___. The ___(4)___ are friendly and I think the ___(5)___ are tasty. Some days, the ___(6)___ let us go ___(7)___. Other days, we have to slip them ___(8)___ in order to go ___(9)___. Best of all, I like the ___(10)___, where I can ___(11)___ all night long if I want. They serve a mean ___(12)___ there. Thanks for the box of ___(13)___ you sent. Those were ___(14)___ and I even gave some to my ___(15)___. I hope ___(16)___ is feeling better. It was shame about the poisoning from ___(17)___. Normally, that material is only found at a ___(18)___, where they frequently use ___(19)___.

I look forward to hearing back from you, maybe even before ___(20)___.

Love, ___(21)___

(1) Member of your family: Mom	(1) Member of your family: Puppy	(1) Member of your family: _____
(2) Member of your family: Dad	(2) Member of your family: Kitty	(2) Member of your family: _____
(3) Place: Scarlet Shores	(3) Place: Kamp Kontainment Zone	(3) Place: _____
(4) Plural Noun: post-lifers	(4) Plural Noun: Horde folks	(4) Plural Noun: _____
(5) Noun: meals	(5) Noun: kounselors	(5) Plural Noun: _____
(6) Plural Noun: guards	(6) Plural Noun: soldiers	(6) Plural Noun: _____
(7) Verb: walking	(7) Verb: wander near the fence	(7) Verb: _____
(8) Plural noun: drug stamps	(8) Plural noun: rocks	(8) Plural noun: _____
(9) Verb: pee	(9) Verb: watch them die	(9) Verb: _____
(10) Place: QCasino	(10) Place: shelter	(10) Place: _____
(11) Activity: gamble	(11) Activity: growl at dirt	(11) Activity: _____
(12) Beverage: Chi-chi	(12) Beverage: green apple martini	(12) Beverage: _____
(13) Food: cookies	(13) Food: entrails	(13) Food: _____
(14) Adjective: yummy	(14) Adjective: slimy	(14) Adjective: _____
(15) Noun: friend	(15) Noun: self	(15) Noun: _____
(16) Person: the plumber	(16) Person: Dr. Beaker	(16) Person: _____
(17) Element from the Periodic Table: argon	(17) Element from the Periodic Table: thallium	(17) Element from the Periodic Table: _____
(18) Type of business: high-end arc welding shop	(18) Type of business: photocell manufacturing plant	(18) Type of business: _____
(19) A size of crescent wrench: 3/8-inch crescent wrenches	(19) A size of crescent wrench: 13/16-inch crescent wrenches	(19) A size of crescent wrench: _____
(20) Holiday: St. Swithin's Day	(20) Holiday: The Martyrdom of the Bab	(20) Holiday: _____
(21) Person: Sally	(21) Person: Li'l Freddie Meep	(21) Person: _____

I'm told we get a lot of questions about our post-lifer dating service, Stiff Competition. You know, that's how I met Doris, and we're as happy as dead clams. Anyway, here's a yarn about S.C. and it's our next episode of...

SCARLET STORIEZ 2:

LOVE IN THE TIME OF P1V1

"Stiff Competition," Jane answered cheerfully, picking up the phone, knocking over her coffee, and cursing under her breath. As usual, there was only a slightly muffled sound on the other end. How can we get them to start talking, she wondered, as she mopped up the spill.

Jane felt a deep sense of responsibility to this "experiment," as her former boss, Larry, called it. About a year ago, Jane was merely a Class 3 Clerk in the D.R.D. (Disaster Recovery Department) of the federal government, working in a dim, grim cubicle in downtown Omaha. Her job was to handle the bulk of paperwork that was generated concerning the numerous post-lifers being resettled to that city's Scarlet Shores Beta. She also handled an obligatory amount of Containment Zone paperwork, which frustrated her because she already didn't have the time or resources to help the lifers, let alone document what became of the "zoners," as they were called. "We've got to cut our losses somewhere," Larry would regularly say.

Then, one day while having a mid-morning bagel in the break room, Jane had the bright idea of trying to assist post-lifers with their social skills. I've seen

them over at the Shores, she thought, and they seem a bit shy. Usually they don't do much more than mill around and stare at each other—it's like a living dead sock hop. What if I could find a way to introduce them to each other?

Hold it, she thought, standing up from the table, jazzed by her idea. What if I could find a way to pair them up? Like a dating service or something of that nature. Wouldn't that be comforting to them? Wouldn't that be *better*?

The idea was a natural and Jane was the perfect person to implement it. For as long as she could remember, she'd been pairing up friends whenever the opportunity arose. She had a genuine knack for it—she'd meet someone new and think, I bet they'd hit it off with so-and-so, and then Jane would arrange for her friends to meet in a quiet cafe or other neutral location. Her batting average was unusually high and now, on occasion, her friends would seek her out, asking if she'd met anyone new.

Believing that she could transform her talent into a service for the post-lifers, Jane spent a couple of days refining her idea and wrote a presentation for her boss. Summoning the nerve, she walked into Larry's office and asked him for a few minutes of his time. When he looked up, she tossed the mini-proposal onto his desk and explained the concept with inspired precision. She went on to tell Larry that she'd even tracked down a funding source through the D.R.D.'s database.

Larry looked at Jane as if she'd made the pitch in a dead language. But just as he was on the verge of dismissing both her and her inane idea, he remembered that Fed memo he'd recently received. It was from the bigwigs and, it seemed that, surprisingly, based on the latest polls and surveys, there was a widespread public perception that simply containing the Disaster and housing the post-lifers wasn't enough. There needed to be more of an effort put forth to make their conditions better. They had been, after all, at one time, someone's mom, baby brother, uncle, or whomever. No uninfected person wanted *their* transformed relative to be mistreated and, in no uncertain terms, had let the bigwigs know.

As a result of this populist push, the Feds were now willing to reward managers for positive, creative ideas that might help achieve that goal and change the public's perception, particularly if it could be done on the cheap. If Jane could pull off this ludicrous concept, Larry schemed, he could take credit and get one of those bonuses. Hell, he'd even share it with her.

So when Larry responded to the proposal with a level of enthusiasm unseen since last year's Christmas party, Jane was more than surprised. He told her how to punch up her proposal and that she should begin making notes on how she'd go about putting the service together. He, in turn, would initiate the process of having her transferred and possibly even upgraded to a higher class level, one that would be outside of her clerk status altogether. Larry figured she'd need to work under the broader canopy of Post-Human Resources, but guessed that wouldn't be an issue. He was sure the Feds would flip for this shit.

So, here was Jane, well into her fifth month in this position she'd created—she *really* was a yenta of sorts now, with two assistants and her own office. She'd had the IT department set her up with a couple of VOIP phone lines the lifers could use to directly contact the agency. As with the National White Courtesy Phone System, no dialing was necessary, which made it considerably more post-lifer friendly. She also had an interactive webcam system set up, and it worked the way Skype once did. When the lifers *did* figure out how to work the webcam (which was hit and miss), they got the chance to talk with someone they could see, which always produced better results.

Currently, there were several commercials for Jane's service running on Scarlet TV, The Pulse, and elsewhere, promoting a cute young couple, Jason and Leah. Of course, they were only actors who'd been made up to resemble lifers. Jane thought the ads were effective and was grateful she'd decided to use a human couple instead of any of the lifer couples they'd considered. "First we have to sell this," she'd said to the ad agency.

Jane maintained a massive bulletin board on one of her office walls where she paired up different photos of lifers who had expressed an interest in meeting each other. The webcam system also gave Jane a better sense of what condition they were in. For example, she wouldn't want to pair up a newbie with a post-lifer who might be mentally and/or physically far more gone; there'd be less chance for success.

The biggest problem so far, though, was getting the lifers to talk on the phone. As Jane had learned the hard way, a post-lifer's attention span was not a thing of beauty and a whole lot worse than she'd been led to believe. With the webcam system, at least, she could keep her clients' attention by providing visual stimuli; with the phone, not as much. Because of the lifer's pervasive ADD, she wasn't getting the results she wanted. But she had no intention of ever returning to the clerk job. She recognized that she needed to be more proactive and decided to take her services directly to the lifers.

Next, Jane arranged for a "Half-Speed Dating" event that she'd host at Scarlet Shores Beta (or just "The Beta" as the locals called it), with tables, soft lighting, and appetizers the clients might enjoy. With the nearly serene atmosphere working in her favor, she could personally oversee the event with the help of Ted and Nancy, her two coworkers, and a lot of extra security. But the bottom line was: she *would* make magic happen.

The night of the big affair, Jane's mind wandered as she made the routine drive to The Beta. She flashed back to how the service was named. "Stiff Competition"— she still wasn't crazy about the choice or how it was foisted upon her. It seemed smarmy to her. A mid-level suit had blurted it out in a strategy session and everyone (but Jane) thought it was enormously clever. You wouldn't think if was so damn cute if you were one of *them*, Jane thought, and made a face. She'd liked her two name ideas more: "The Love of Your Post-Life" or "Couple Up!" Neither, however, went over well and the suit's idea stuck.

As Jane pulled into the parking area, she realized The Beta never ceased to amaze her. It felt as if it had always been there, and yet the structure was less than six years old. The Beta looked like it had organically sprouted right out of the shoreline—a humungous, shiny white boat-shaped object with few windows and an impossibly smooth surface. Jane flashed back on the thousands of construction workers that had converged on the site shortly after the first wave of the Disaster and remembered how there had actually been *nothing* organic about it.

Once Jane parked and endured the multiple layers of security to gain admittance to the building, she found Ted and Nancy had not only arrived, but had already set up tables and chairs, put out the appetizers, hung cheery signs, and even arranged for the Shores' kitchen staff to provide a sizeable bowl of punch for the gathering. Jane glanced at the punch and wondered about the pinkish chunks that floated in it. She started to ask a staffer, but decided against it. Shake it off, she thought, you don't need to know *everything*.

At five o'clock on the nose, the lifers began to slowly wander in. As they amassed inside, the additional security made themselves more visible, which Jane thought was a bit much. Totalitarian romance, she reflected.

Jane had been around the lifers on and off but, she had to confess, it was still a bit jarring every time she saw them. Still, she thought, they're much better off than the Horde populace. At least here they can have a chance at an existence that included the generous stamp programs and at *least* three square meals a day. And with that last reflection, the event officially began.

Two hours later, Jane pushed herself away from her hosting table feeling both satisfaction *and* frustration. There had been more chaos than she'd anticipated. For example, the entire first hour had been spent trying to get the lifers to understand the nature of the event; that had taken a lot of wind out of the collective sails of Ted, Nancy, and Jane. However, once the three of them got the "Half-Speed Dating" concept across to their audience, the event went as well as could be expected, especially for a first time. About a dozen "humpers" (as the security detail called them) had to be broken up, several scuffles broke out over who would sit where, and the punch ran out too early, which caused a few hurt feelings.

Nevertheless, after comparing notes with her staff and the workers at the Shores, Jane was convinced they'd made a grand total of seven matches. And not all of them were even hetero; the concept of even trying to monitor the sexual preferences of the lifer population was laughable to Jane. Let them do whatever they'd like, she thought, as she watched a newly formed female couple saunter out of the meeting room, lovingly touching and sniffing each other.

In that moment, Jane was positive she'd found her niche in life. "Love *is* the answer," she said aloud, packing up her laptop and putting on her coat, not realizing that, at that same moment, Ted was being violently attacked in a nearby men's room by an improperly medicated pair of post-lifers, and wouldn't be found until it was far too late.

QUIZZZTIME!!!: LOVE IN THE TIME OF P1V1

Please circle the correct answers.

Yeah, like you didn't cheat before: page 101.

1.	Jane is kinda like a pimp. True False		5.	S.S. Beta is a picturesque place. True False
2.	Larry likes to drink at Christmas. True False		6.	Humpers are cool. True False
3.	Ted and Nancy are good workers. True False		7.	Chunks make punch sillier. True False
4.	Ted and Nancy are having an affair. True False		8.	The life of a Class 3 Clerk sucks. True False

Dr. Kenneth Beaker, PhD, Scientist, and Humanitarian, would have a word with you...

Actually it's more like **ten** words!
One letter is missing in each of the words below.
How hard can it be? Really.
Let's goose that QScale number!

Answers on page 101.

FEMOR__L	SWOLL__N
INFE__TION	PITU__TARY
OBLO__GATA	MUCU__
C__NVULSIONS	CRANI__M
OWWWWW__	ACKKKKFF__

DO *YOU* NEED TO RE-LEARN *English?*

If so, we hope you'll let *Roberta Stone* assist you in mastering language once more.

Roberta Stone is the official educational language system of the Steak Department, the President's Council on Fitness and Chips, and what was once lightheartedly referred to as "The United Nations." The *Roberta Stone* system has a proven track record based on its seventeen-point "redundancy to the point of exhaustion" principles, as well as *Roberta's* monotone, grating, nasally voice. Accordingly, you'll want to get through these fourteen discs as quickly as possible. You'll be up and not understanding what you're saying in no time flat.

How does the system work? Pop in one of the CDs, sit back and get ready to learn at an incredibly rapid rate. Soon, after the agitation passes, you'll be the envy of your friends, using flashy words like "fern " and "at"!

Available in English, Spanish, Esperanto, Cockney, and Urban Urdu.

For details, call 1-877-555-1400 x57248, ask for Juan or, if Juan isn't there, ask for Sayid but, really, either of them is cool. But be sure to use the codeword "orator" or Sayid will get cheesed.

Roberta Stone—**talk the talk.**

I'm on my way!

Answers on page 101.

Dr. Doofus, ORGAN DETECTIVE!

Paging Dr. Doofus, paging Dr. Doofus! Code Red in the Hall of Fixins! Unidentified organs have appeared at a table and we need you STAT!

Hi, kidz. **Dr. Doofus**, ORGAN DETECTIVE, here.

I get calls like this all the time—random organs showing up in the darndest places. When that happens, it's up to me to identify those organs and *pronto*!

Here are my last five cases. I cracked 'em all. How about you?

MYSTERY ORGAN	Solution?
	Why Dr., I believe that's a _____!
	No doubt about it, sir, you've got yourself a genuine _____!

MYSTERY ORGAN	Solution?
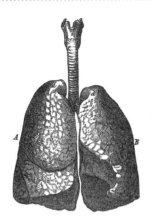	I can tell you one thing, ma'am: that's a nice set of _____ you've got there!
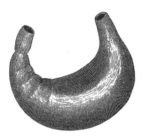	I'm sorry, Ms. Grey, but "banana" is not the correct answer. The correct answer is _____!
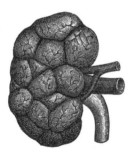	Gotta tell ya, I rarely see these suckers in the wild. Whatcha got right here is a truly splendid example of a _____!

How'd that work out for ya? Ackkfffff!

Senator Frederick Meep

DISCUSSES HIS USE OF

FAUXTOX™:

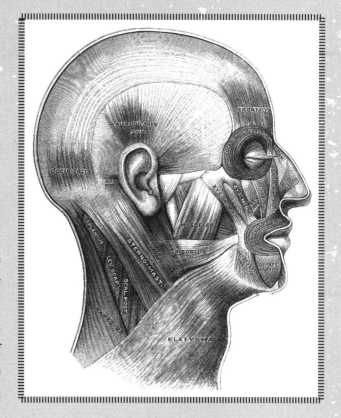

I represent the biggest remaining state in our union and my constituency expects me to always look my best. That's why recently I listened when one of my mistresses began talking about how much she was enjoying her **FAUXTOX** treatments.

FAUXTOX isn't just for post-lifers anymore. That's right—perfectly normal people like myself, the Speaker of the Hose, the Minority Whippet, and many, many more now depend on this fantastic product to help keep us looking smooth and vigorous.

A simple, weekly gargantuan shot does it all. And yes, it can be painful as hell, but it's completely worth it.

I can't begin to tell you the number of compliments I get. My kids think I look young and my wife, Janice, even made a nice remark. Let me tell you, that's *really* saying something because we hardly speak anymore!

So, here's my advice: Don't let anyone or anything get between you and how you *could* look. This election season and every day gauxing forward—

Gaux **FauxTox!**

"♫ Get the Most Life from Your Post-Life With ♫

QualiCola®"

Please give a **BIG** welcome the latest member of our product line—*Cherry QC*!

QualiCola or *DietQualiCola*

or *Cherry QualiCola*

—*As real as you are!*

Paper Dolls, Part One: *The Doris Portfolio*

It never lets up for the darling Doris. Today, she makes a cameo appearance as a celebrity cheerleader for a charity fundraiser and then she's off to a high-profile masquerade ball, where she'll be going as a glamorous, deceased beauty queen. That girl is livin' the high post-life!

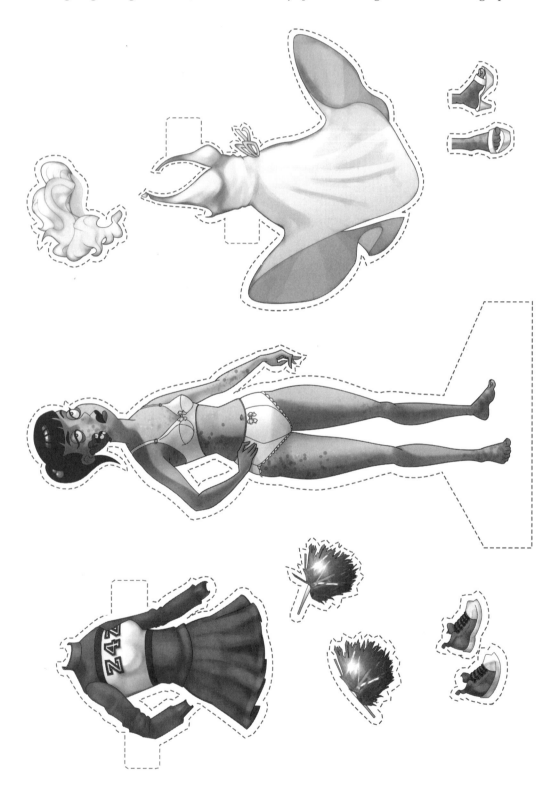

Paper Dolls, Part Two: *THE DOOFUS PORTFOLIO*

It's a big day for Doof, too. He's got a gig in a commercial shoot for a certain "fruity" underwear manufacturer, followed by an invite to a boat christening. Good thing he's got the gear!

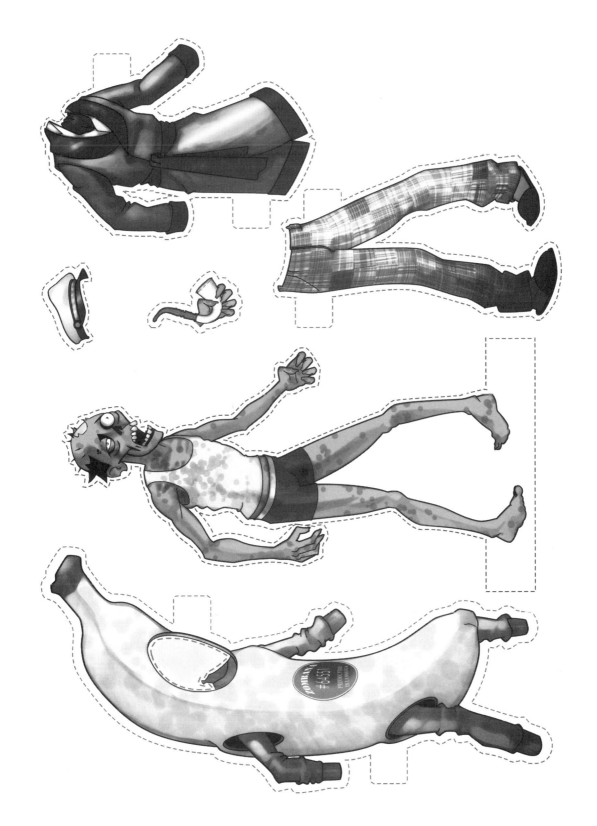

Jeepers, who doesn't enjoy a fine game of Jamble? Can *you* solve this? Did your CareBox arrive yet?

PRODUCTIVA PRESENTS:

JAMBLE —THAT PAIN-IN-THE-ASS MIXED-UP WORD GAME!

Answers on page 101.

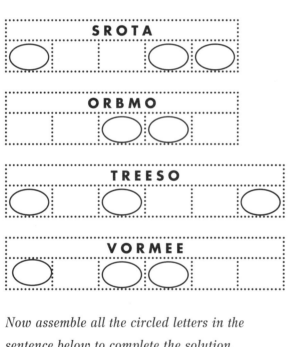

SROTA

ORBMO

TREESO

VORMEE

Now assemble all the circled letters in the sentence below to complete the solution. (*What a pain in the ass.*)

What Chomps said as he ordered from the fast-food drive-thru lane.

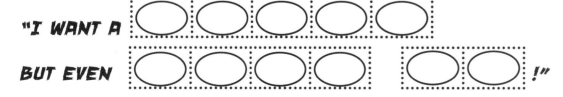

"I WANT A ⬭⬭⬭⬭⬭

BUT EVEN ⬭⬭⬭⬭ ⬭⬭ !"

SUNDAEZ OF THE GODZ!

We asked you to send in ideas about what you'd consider your dream ice cream sundae. Boy howdy, did you ever come through! A few of these sound almost edible!

Free-Range Feast

I was only free range for a day before my parents found me and somehow got me into the Shores. My dad probably bribed someone—what a douche. Anyway, before I got nabbed, I found this bitchin' old farmhouse where some major shit must've gone down. The place was littered with the bodies of cops and Horde guys alike. I felt like I'd walked into my ideal diorama. Happily, I found some ice cream in the freezer and a bunch of toppings to go with it and had myself one heck of a feast. I'll spare you the details, but I will say this: Banana Skull Split.

Tad Moot, Jr., age 17

Sneeze Surprise

Speech really isn't my thing, so meeting new people can be difficult for me. To get around that shortcoming, I've learned to break the ice with a little gift. In this case, something sweet. I prepare a delicious-looking hot fudge sundae, sneeze on it several times, then give it away to a passing stranger. Pretty soon, I've made a new friend.

Jiffy, no age listed

Frozen Siren of Desire

Why do you call to me and how
do you have this affect upon me
you are only a freezer and yet
I am powerless to resist your siren sounds.
You say, come take from me this cold sweet carton
and I have no will.
I grab a bowl from a stack of bowls and begin.
Later, in the melty afterglow, I will feel dirty
and ashamed
but for now
I am that which you have given me:
dulce de leche and a reason to live one more day.

Bamboo Reed,
author of The Tao of Scarlet Shores

Mt. Cottonball

What I do, which is very popular with me, is obtain a very large bowl and fill it with 5 or 6 scoops of the vanilla flavor of the ice cream product I enjoy. Then over there by the dessert bar they let me use more chocolate sauce than I should and I give the ice cream I enjoy a good coat or two. Then over there by the dessert bar I put some jimmies on it but then—and here's the special part—I pull several cottonballs out of my pocket and place them on the mound of ice cream and chocolate sauce and, after positioning them in a pleasing way, it is followed by the eating of it all.

Manny Cottonball, Age 43

Trundle Mint Twist

My dream sundae is 2 scoops of mint chip ice cream with a cup of ground Trundle mixed in. Stir briskly until it's all mixed together really well. And be sure you eat it quickly before the Trundle starts to brown and coagulate, because then it gets this troubling film all over it and becomes even less appetizing. Doesn't taste great either.

Danny, age 14

And finally, Horny, the living dead unicorn, was kind enough to weigh in:

Sugar 'n Spice

M-m-mine's pretty s-simple: Dump a p-pint of B-b-black Ch-cherry Psychosis in a b-bowl, add 3 c-carrots, and t-top it w-with sssssugar c-c-c-cubes. It's t-t-terrif!

Horny

BRIDGE

A few of you asked for a Bridge column, but I have no idea why.
I mean, even folks with perfectly good minds struggle with this "yuppity" game.
If this lesson makes any sense to you, then bully.

Really? You're gonna play Bridge?? This I gotta see!!

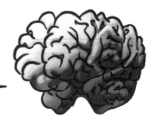

South is vulnerable and subject to crying jags. North sighs heavily and deals.

NORTH
♠ 6
♥ Q 5
♦ K J 10 2 9
♣ 9 6 2 4 K

WEST
♠ 4 8 5
♥ 8 7 K J
♦ 3 7 8 Q
♣ 8 3

EAST
♠ 2 7 Q K A
♥ 2 4 6
♦ 4 5 6
♣ 5 7 10

SOUTH
♠ 3 9 10 J
♥ 3 9 10 A
♦ A
♣ J Q A

The bidding:

WEST	NORTH	EAST	SOUTH
3 ♠ *	2 ♠ *	4 ♠	3 ♠*
Pass	Pass		Pass
(*feeble)	(*misguided)		(*nice blouse)

Opening lead: Ace of ♠

Consider the spade suit in the East-West hands. Are you seeing what I'm seeing? I see a certain holy figure in the pattern—do you? No? Uhhh—awkward. Okay then, what suit would you need to play in order to avoid a hissy fit?

East had a difficult bidding problem, which may have to do with his "daddy issues." West was unsure how East might treat him, so he was appropriately aloof during the auction. Declarer led with a Joker, mugged at the other three players, and considered himself to be quite the kidder. Hilarity came nowhere near ensuing.

After the yelling stopped, South led with the ace of clubs and then, as she grinded her gears, downshifted to a heart. Declarer then picked up the heart and explained how the word "dummy" is used in bridge, which seemed sort of snooty if you asked me. After the overly lengthy explanation and elaborate slideshow, North was still confused and kept asking when the ventriloquist would arrive.

Inexplicably, after the king of diamonds was played, East yelled "Gin."

Meanwhile, if West saw that trumps were 4–2, and all distributions and combinations were off the table, then there would be no need for either the doubleton ace or that Montag gal.

North was encouraged to force his strong hand of clubs onto the group, while simultaneously being advised that he might want to consider simpler hobbies, such as bug collecting. Obviously, South stood a better chance of winning in this case because of her "long call" in both spades and February Red Wheat, not to mention the distraction to the other players of her low-cut diaphanous blouse.

When West swipes the final nine of hearts from the "Pile o' Doom" (this approach is recommended only for advanced players), North should be able to step in, win the hand, and hopefully this time not say something hurtful like "Snap!" or "Take that, losers."

South will start to weep once more, but soon will be comforted by West with an available strong shoulder and a bottle of shitty white zin. This will eventually lead to poor decision-making and, ultimately, break up the foursome.

(Bridge is brought to you by Mr. William Feldstein, Grandmaster Poobah and contributing writer for QualiCorps Media Services and *QualiLife* magazine. If you have any questions regarding this lesson, Mr. Feldstein would greatly appreciate it if you keep them to yourselves. Thank you.)

THIS DAY IN **HISTORY:**

1860: Last day of service for the ill-conceived competitor to the Pony Express, "The Phony Express," which service consisted of two men in a horse suit. "What it lacked in efficiency, it more than made up for in mirth," said defiant founder Robert "Buck" McMillan at the closing ceremonies.

1902: Cyrus Pinkerton's play, "Yankee in a Hoop Skirt," opened in London and closed the next day due to a suspicious theatre fire. Both the skirt and its understudy perished in the blaze.

1921: Nothing special.

1945: The World Bank was created by twenty-eight nations, nine of whom immediately defaulted.

1971: Aliens land and, after making first contact in Washington, DC, decide it wasn't such a swell idea and promptly leave.

2001: Unusually dull day. Still no monolith.

2012: Mayans are proven to be jittery wankers.

2018: Work begins on constructing the first Containment Zone. It is quickly determined that a chain-link fence is not gonna cut it. No duh.

DOUBLE CROZZWERDZ!!

So now every word has *double* z's? What is *wrong* with you?

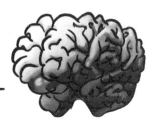

This'll jack up your awesome thinky powers!

Answers on page 102.

ACROSS

Open-air area for goombahs (6)

What the Americans always frickin' order in the above location (5)

Valley-speak for severe wintr'y conditions (9)

Messed-up-lookin' old dude's face (8)

What hair you have left might be getting this way (6)

Was he _____ re bear? (5)

Drank like a frat boy (7)

DOWN

What this might qualify as, like, a game (6)

Vertigo effect/Tommy Roe (5)

Ancient bearded TX rockers (5)

High, Lightyear, or Aldrin (4)

To make anxious, jittery (7)

Heckle or poor "berry" partner (4)

To amaze/overwhelm, but not in this book (6)

What her friends called the adult Borden girl (4)

GOT A MATCH?

The names of eight different anti-Horde weapons have been mixed up.
Put the correct halves with one another.

Answers on page 102.

1. Super lemurs   _____
2. Laser pluggo   _____
3. Particle fork   _____
4. Atom shears   _____
5. Molecular scrambler   _____
6. Vibro mitt   _____
7. Dimensional hammer   _____
8. Robot catapult   _____

THE MYSTIC OMAR DOOFUS, SUB-MENTALIST, SAYS:

Here's a wonderful trick I learned as a child while working the streets of Bombay. Ackfff.

I'VE GOT YOUR NUMBER!

Pick any number.

Add 7, then divide by 2.

Add 26 and multiply by 3.

Divide by 1.67 and then add 4.

The resulting number will have ABSOLUTELY NOTHING to do with your original number.

The Mystic Omar Doofus astounds you once more!

WERD SURCH 2

If you sucked last time, here's your chance to redeem me!

A Phil Shortz original. Answers on page 102.

```
T  G  G  N  A  S  H  M  H  F
G  R  U  N  T  S  S  A  F  L
V  I  U  D  D  L  L  G  S  A
Q  N  R  N  E  E  A  G  H  T
V  D  V  W  D  L  T  O  U  L
E  E  O  Z  U  L  H  T  F  I
N  R  Z  U  T  U  E  S  F  N
T  T  O  R  C  H  R  O  L  E
R  Z  N  Z  H  H  Z  P  E  M
I  V  E  L  B  U  R  P  D  M
C  I  B  L  I  S  S  I  U  M
L  L  O  I  N  F  E  C  T  S
E  L  U  N  G  E  S  W  A  T
K  J  C  H  O  M  P  S  B  B
```

Can YOU find these hidden werdz?

TORCH	GRUNTS	MAGGOTS	OUCH
FLATLINE	GNASH	VENTRICLE	INFECTS
SLATHER	SHUFFLED	SCAB	BLISSIUM
LUNGES	TRUNDLE	GRINDER	LOIN
BURP	DUTCH BINGO	CHOMPS	ZONE
POST	TROWEL	UHH	SWAT

(Remember to check the diagonals, too!)

THE FOOD YOU MADE

Today, we've got two dope dishes. Keep sending us those fly recipes and keep munching, bruh. Peace.

Sally, from Scarlet Shores Jr. in Omaha, writes:

My friend Jiffy sure enjoys these sandwiches when I'm allowed to visit him. I think Elvis did, too. When do I get to go home?

Peanut Butter 'N Cranial Jelly Sammich

3 tsps. QualiKo Knutty Butter Pee-knut Product
2 tsps. Gristle's-To-Go Cranial Jelly (w/Omega 3)
2 slices of bread
1 pat of butter

Spread butter on bread. Spread peanut butter on bread. Spread cranial jelly on bread. Give it to Jiffy. Cry.

Manny Cottonball sent us his fave and says:

I like this it's got cotton balls.

Cotton Balls in Oil

10–12 cotton balls, any brand
4 tbsps. olive oil, any brand
Salt and pepper

Pour the oil in the thing that holds the stuff and then put cotton balls in there and allow them to marinate in the thing with the oil for 5 minutes the way I enjoy them and then salt and pepper and eat them.

"I'll teach YOU how to HYPNOTIZE anyone within 23 minutes!"

My given name is Ira Owens, but you can call me HypnoMaster, Master of the Hypnotic. I've been studying the mysterious world of hypnotism for years, and recently ascended to the position of "Fourth Level Master," which you probably do *not* realize is a very huge deal.

I'm here to share with you the knowledge that few have ever known or ever wanted to know. The power I'm offering you is astonishing. Tell me, would you like to:

- ⊙ Get any gal, any guy, anywhere at any time?
- ⊙ Have complete strangers give you cash?
- ⊙ See your QScale number shoot up off the charts?
- ⊙ Never have to pay for another meal?
- ⊙ Get all the stamp books you *ever* wanted?

The truth is, post-life can sap self-confidence and enthusiasm out of the best of us. Don't let that happen to YOU. My program, "23 Minutes or Less," **will** give you command over *your* world *and the worlds of others*.

Just so you know, if I wanted to, I could hypnotize every reader right now and force you to accept this offer. It would be the best thing that ever happened to you. But I won't do that and you know why? Because it would go against *The Code* and the Fifth Level guys would seriously jump down my throat.

However, if you **do** want to have the most remarkable post-life possible and realize **all** of your dreams, then call me at 1-877-NOD-U-OUT. Send no money—I'll come by to collect it personally. And no, I don't take checks. You WILL give me cash (or stamps, if need be).

Sincerely,
Ira Owens
but you can call me
HypnoMaster, Master of the Hypnotic

CRYPTIC CLUSTERFUN

> Don't ask me!!

Be warned: this is, without a doubt, the most difficult puzzle in the book. And for the record, no one has ever solved a single one of these because they make no sense. That said, rotsa ruck!

Here's how it works: Each clue has two parts: numerical and literary. The top row is the numerical half, which may or may not represent the letters contained in each final answer. Once the numerical half is decoded, the result may very well need to be thrown out OR combined with the seemingly total gibberish of the literary half. Each literary clue may involve double definitions, anagrams, split words, homophones, mobile phones, hidden clues, reclining nudes, backward every-other-letter logic, full-cavity searches, high colonics, occasional spasms, or NOT. Each answer then serves as a clue to the TREMENDOUSLY BIG BONUS ANSWER (the "TBBA") at the tail end of this mess.

Answers on page 103.

A. 23 1 17 12 5 6 9
Talking toupee on the Munchkin Mayor's head of lettuce alone?

__ ___ _____ ____ _

B. 14 11 2 19 8 8 8 8 8
The gerbils have gone over their text limit for the month and Gaga-ed the tamale.

_____

C. 26 15 19 2 16 9 3 17 1 17 1 3 3 2
Vandalism prism in the windmills of your mineshaft (just talkin' 'bout Shaft).

_____ __ ___ _____

D. 7 3 9 11 25
Dangerous fiancée with a pill-box hat and a blank note from her doctor, Phil.

__ _____ ____ _

E. 19
General Tso's Chicken-Fried ambassador to Peru in another Lifetime channel commercial?

____ _____

F. 23 1 17 12 5 6 9
Gandhi's deodorant clam bake sale hubris

_____ ____ _____

THE TREMENDOUSLY BIG BONUS ANSWER:

A–F plus:	
Garden of Eden sub-reference, page 32, para. 3, line 8 of Milton's missing journal and sandwich delivery menu for the greater Cambridge area coo coo kachoo	___ _____ __ _____ _____

THE DEAD BEAR FAMILY

Join us as we visit that loveable bunch, Sleazy (the papa bear), Weezy (the mama bear), Breezy (the prissy girl cub), and Cheezy (the moronic boy cub). What's that? It seems there's some sort of commotion in the home of The Dead Bear Family...

WEEZY: Father, I will not allow you to bring that beehive into this den!

SLEAZY: Damn it, Weezy! I don't have much choice—it's stuck on my head!

BREEZY: Daddy said a bad word!

CHEEZY: Damn straight, sis!

WEEZY: Now look what you've done, Sleazy—Junior's learned a bad word.

SLEAZY: What the hell do I care? As I *said*, there's a freakin' beehive stuck on my head and these little bastards are stinging me like all get out!! *Hello?* I'm in pain *over here*!

BREEZY: Oh, my poor little girl ears!

CHEEZY: This is great; I'm learning more words here than at The Bear Academy!

WEEZY: That's it, Father! You take off that ridiculous hive hat, step outside, and don't you come back until you've calmed down. The Dead Bear Family does not conduct itself in such a coarse manner.

SLEAZY: Grumble, grumble, mumble, grumble.

BREEZY: Mommy, am I a bastard?

WEEZY: Honey, that's a conversation we don't need to have right now.

CHEEZY: Hell, I wouldn't even mind it if I'm a damn freakin' bastard!

WEEZY AND BREEZY: CHEEZY!!!

Put 'Em Back Together, Willya?

Ten 6-letter words were horsing around in a ShuffleCraft and, when they fell out of the vehicle, they broke in half. Once they've been correctly reassembled, all ten will be objects you'd find at Gristle's After Dark Adult Drinkatorium. Use the right-hand columns to put 'em back together, willya?

What a forced setup!

Answers on page 103.

DAN	ERS	CHO	ICE	_____	_____
POL	ELY	IES	JAE	_____	_____
LAD	CER	DRU	COS	_____	_____
RES	LIF	WHO	NKS	_____	_____
GER	MPS	MOS	LON	_____	_____

Speaking of GRISTLE's—have you tried the savory goodness of the latest culinary hit from Mack's House of Meats, now being served at GRISTLE's?

IT'S THE TRUNDLE ROAST.

It's not pork, it sure isn't chicken, it doesn't come from the ocean, and no way in hell it's beef! It's Trundle and we promise you've never had any *thing* like it.

To experience the greatest taste sensation to sweep the remaining States, come to GRISTLE's for **THE TRUNDLE ROAST.**

Experience whatever it is tonight.

Don't forget: Tuesday through Thursday nights are "Ladies' Night" at Gristle's After Dark.
Half-price drink specials for all gals, cross-dressers, or gender-confused from 5 'til closing.

Dudes and Dudesses, are you ready to shred? Too bad—we're gonna crank it anyway! In this YO installment, we feature Timmy, a lively lad who's like a cross between a newborn colt and a crackhead. Let's see what happens to him in our latest episode of **Scarlet Storiez**...

SCARLET STORIEZ 3:

A ZOMBIE WALK FOR TIMMY

It was mid-October and Timmy was as stoked as could be. He'd been crossing off the days on his calendar for two whole weeks and there were no days left. The big one had finally arrived—today, with his dad and Uncle Ned, Timmy was going to his first zombie walk.

Until most recently, Timmy didn't even know what a zombie walk was. Timmy's dad had come home several Wednesdays ago (as he did every Wednesday) with a bag full of new comic books. Only *this* time, when Timmy was going though the

stack, sneaking peeks at the ones his dad wouldn't let him read, Timmy discovered a flyer had been included in the bag. It read: "Come one, come all! Bring out ye dead and make 'em walk! Zombie Walk, October 17, 2:00 p.m., Ragnaröckers, 13724½ Ventura Boulevard, Sherman Oaks. Prizes for best costumes and best makeup!"

As soon as he saw the word "prizes," Timmy's eyes lit up as if they were battery-powered. He asked his dad what a zombie walk was and his father, while scanning the new issue of *Captain Marmoset*, told him that a zombie walk is a giant party where people make themselves up to resemble zombies. Just like those cool folks in the otherwise lame Lutheran haunted house, Timmy thought. Everyone dresses up in funny clothes, his dad added, and wanders around a nearby residential neighborhood, talking and acting like zombies.

Well, that sounded like the finest thing Timmy'd ever heard of. He immediately begged his dad to do the walk with him on the 17th, to which his dad responded he'd have to "check with the ex." Timmy's mom lived on the other side of the hill with her most recent husband, Ron, whose face looked like it was on too tight. And now Timmy's mom's face was looking like that, too.

A couple of days later, Timmy's dad said he'd gotten permission from Timmy's mom and the zombie walk was officially a "go." Timmy's dad explained that they'd need to start working on their makeup and putting their costumes together soon. Timmy's dad revealed that Uncle Ned would be joining them, too. Timmy winced at that bit of news—Uncle Ned was a major dork who said and did screwy things but always treated Timmy nicely. Anyway, Timmy wouldn't allow that to darken his mood; he was as tickled as the time when he forgot to pay for a ball of bubblegum and found it in his pants pocket the next morning.

Timmy and his father enjoyed a great couple of weeks as they prepared for the walk. One day, after his dad got home from work, the two of them went to the thrift store and bought a stack of cheap, strange clothes. They took the garments home, cut a few holes in them, then splattered them with red tempera paint. Last time they'd had this much fun was when dad sneaked Timmy into a strip club.

Via the Internet, Timmy's dad had also tracked down several web pages that offered homemade zombie makeup tips, so they went to Ralph's and purchased what they needed. His dad had enthused at length that they had to look the part. Upon further reflection, Timmy realized that his dad's long-winded enthusiasm most likely had more to do with the Blue Stripe vodka.

The night before the walk, the two stayed up late, perfecting their makeup together and practicing frightening faces in front of the cracked mirror. They both thought they looked pretty awesome. His dad's dead construction worker costume was terrific, complete with a blood-spattered yellow hard hat. Timmy was going as a zombie safety patrol kid. The first time he saw himself in the mirror wearing the torn orange vest, he just about croaked.

The rest of the evening was spent with father and son stumbling around the apartment, growling and grimacing at each other. It was all perfect, except when the phone rang and his dad got into a fight with Louise, his dad's girlfriend. Timmy had never heard his father use those kinds of words before.

The next morning, Timmy got up early, made his bed, helped with the dishes, and did everything he could to make sure his dad would be in better spirits and that they'd have a swell time together on the walk. Timmy was so blissed-out he even made a point not to roll his eyes when Uncle Ned showed up (of course) in a Dracula costume. What a maroon, thought Timmy.

By the time they got made up and dressed up, it was well past one in the afternoon; Timmy was getting anxious. "C'mon, Dad, we've gotta go," Timmy pleaded. "The walk starts at two."

Finally, all three of them climbed into his dad's car and, during the drive, got the funniest looks from people in other cars. Some folks honked their horns, while others yelled out their windows. An old man in a crosswalk even did a double take, nearly fell down, and made Timmy laugh so hard he thought he'd peed his pants. That was close, thought Timmy, after he searched his zombie pants for wet spots.

When they arrived at Ragnaröckers, there must have been hundreds of people there; each of them looked wonderfully awful and creepy. Timmy was dizzy with delight, at least for a moment. He then spotted a few other kids—their makeup looked lousy compared to Timmy's. "Losers," he muttered to himself.

Timmy walked along with his dad, checking out all the zombies and giggling at the costumes. There were dozens of different themes: nightmarish nurses, frightening firemen, a pair of messed-up policemen, and even a woman in a nun's outfit who appeared to have a nice-sized wound on her face. "Hey lady," Timmy said to her, "that's a sweet wound."

But Timmy's favorite costume was a simple one worn by a nearby man. He had on numerous layers of bright, mismatched clothing: stripes, polka dots, and plaids, as well as shirts over shirts. This reminded Timmy of how his dad's cousin dressed—the one who, as a kid, had been kicked in the head by a pony at a petting zoo.

But it wasn't only this guy's costume that was so striking—his makeup was flat-out amazing. It really *did* look like part of his nose was missing and an entire ear, too. There was so much wrong with his face that Timmy couldn't take it all in. I've gotta check this guy out, thought Timmy. So after getting his dad's okay to briefly explore the store on his own, Timmy sought out the colorfully dressed fellow and tapped him on the leg.

"Hey, I just want to tell you your makeup should win the prize! And your costume, too. It's cool!"

The man slowly looked down at Timmy, half smiled at him, grunted, and nodded. I bet this schmuck got kicked by a pony, too, thought Timmy.

"Put 'er there, sir," Timmy said, offering his hand. "You're the winner in my book!"

As they shook hands, Timmy became even more impressed with what this guy had achieved with his costume. The stranger's hand was cold and clammy, and Timmy wondered how he did that. Ice in his pants? Right about then, Timmy noticed the guy's badly smudged name tag that read: "Hello, my name is Jiffy."

"Well, Mr. Jiffy, good luck to ya!" Timmy said as he turned to walk away. "I've gotta get back to my dad."

Timmy caught up with his father just as everyone was lining up for the walk. Timmy, his dad, and Ned were near the end of the line, which was neat because Timmy had a better view of all the zombies. He noticed the Mr. Jiffy guy appeared to be swaying back and forth while he waited for the walk to begin. Looks like he's warming up his engine, Timmy observed.

As the line moved out the door toward Ventura Boulevard, Timmy's dad reminded both Uncle Ned and himself about staying together *and* of the proper way to shamble. It was important to move slowly, drag your feet a little, while throwing in the proper amount of staggering to keep it real. By now, Timmy was so jacked up he felt as if his head was about to explode. He was sorry he'd sneaked in that energy drink with lunch.

The walk was proceeding in an orderly manner as the group wandered into a residential neighborhood, one block south of Ventura. Timmy could see people peeking through their blinds as the long, wobbling crowd passed home after overpriced home. There was a good deal of laughter, groaning, and cutting up going on within the group. Even his Uncle Ned was doing a better-than-dorky job—though a vampire looked like a nerd next to zombies.

Suddenly, Timmy heard someone screaming and looked over to see Mr. Jiffy hugging a zombie nurse. It looked like they were kissing, but she was yelling and fake blood was streaming out what looked like a hole in her neck. Everyone chuckled as the crowd passed by them. Nice neck effect, thought Timmy. Dad and I will have to figure that one out.

As Timmy continued to watch the couple, the zombie lady broke away from Jiffy and ran down a nearby alley, back toward the boulevard. Straightening himself and wiping the fake blood off his face, Mr.

Jiffy turned, hissed at the crowd, and shot Timmy a look that was both scary and hilarious. "He's quite the actor," Timmy said to his dad, as they watched Jiffy run toward the alley in pursuit of his nurse friend.

Boy oh boy, I already can't wait 'til next year, thought Timmy, as the sounds of sirens got closer and the nearby screams became ever more faint.

QUIZZZTIME!!!: A ZOMBIE WALK FOR TIMMY

Please circle the correct answers.

I'm not even gonna say it—well, okay—cheater: page 103.

1. Timmy is kind of a judgmental asshat.
   True   False

2. Timmy's mom got remarried to one of those nip and tuck guys.
   True   False

3. Ponies are dangerous.
   True   False

4. Kids love strip clubs.
   True   False

5. This is that same Jiffy guy from the other story, right?
   True   False

6. You *really* had to use the same character again?
   True   False

7. So the book's like, what, halfway done, and you've already run out of ideas?
   True   False

8. I want my money back.
   True   False

RHYMEZ WITH ?????

Finish the sentence with a rhyming word
(but try not to uze all the cluez)!

1. It's best for lunch to have something with a _ _ _ _ _ _.

2. Don't shake or shiver but I think that's your _ _ _ _ _.

3. I don't know where you've been but I'm losing my _ _ _ _.

4. We might need bibs if we're going to have _ _ _ _.

5. He's one of those breeds who constantly _ _ _ _ _ _.

You really need the answers for this one? Whoa. See page 103.

CLUEZ

1. The sound a skull makes; Captain _____?; fallen leaves might also make this sound when you walk in the woods. (And you're out in the woods, WHY?)

2. What am I, chopped _____?; a pleasing blue-plate special; life is to lifer as live is to _____?

3. Kafka Booths help grow your _____?; rind; snakes and Pelosi shed this.

4. Rack of _____?; pulled from Adam (plural) to create a dame; should NEVER be used with "Mc."

5. Has to do with what #3 holds in; let it _____?; food is to feeds as blood is to _____?

Oh, One Of Those "WHICH IS NOT THE SAME" Things, RIGHT?

Right. Find the object in each row that's considerably more dim-witted than the others.

SHOP BY MAIL! SHOP BY PHONE!

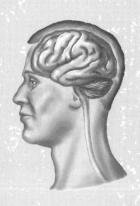

Who would want to take a ride with someone like HIM?

What?

I'm Dean Wright and it's exactly because of folks like Doofus that I started The ShuffLimo Transportation Company. With the ShuffLimo service, you'll no longer have to endure the boorish behavior of the riffraff. For a small Drug Stamp charge, you can be on your way today to the destination of your choice, reclining in the posh, quiet comfort of a ShuffLimo.

We'll pick you up at the curb of your choice and there's a strong likelihood we'll drop you off later at the very same place! What that means for you is—

- ⊙ No more long waits for the Crafts with bums and loiterers.
- ⊙ No more awkward silences with your low-level fellow residents.
- ⊙ No more missing the handrail and falling to the ground.
- ⊙ No more 19/6 for YOU.
- ⊙ No more accidentally sitting in drool.

Call us and experience a ride of unparalleled luxury.

Let The ShuffLimo Transportation Company take you where you need to go.

Unlike our competitor, we're available on Sundays and every day between 1 and 6 a.m.

1-877-SHUFLME

TRIVI-UHHH QUIZZZ!!

Answers on page 103.

1. There are ten human body parts that are only three letters long—eye, hip, arm, and leg are four. What are the rest?

2. Name three Containment Zones west of the Rockies.

3. After the U.S. was infected, what were the next countries to be overwhelmed by the P1V1 Disaster?

4. According to the fine print on the CereBella packaging, avoid doing what while taking the drug?

5. Can you come up with all the different stamp programs in ten seconds or less? Go!

6. Once you enlist in the Paraguard, your first tour of duty lasts how long?

7. Ben walked seven blocks to get to the friendly, neighborhood QualiKo store. How far did Ben walk?

8. Does this Buk ever seem like it's just one continuous ad for crap?

9. Your buddy, Rob, tells you he's going on a trip to Japan. What's wrong with his statement?

10. Without looking, can you spell "broccoflower?"

Yo, nimrod— do I have to tell you *everything*? Make an effort!

LET'S PLAY "FOREST BINGO!"

"Forest Bingo?" you ask. No, it's not the name of your President's younger brother. This is a game that resembles the screwball "Auto Bingo" game we played in our youth. (Well, you older folks might remember Auto Bingo in a distant analog time before there were multiple DVD screens in everyone's family vehicle. I mean, how many times can kids actually watch those films? Talk about *zombies*!)

Where was I? Ah yes, next time you're out wandering in the woods when you're not supposed to be, take a friend and these two cards along. See who completes their card first!

FOREST BINGO
CARD #1

	Empty quart of Pabst	Chomps the Clown, roughing up someone		Druids around a campfire
Crumpled copy of *The Watchtower*		Spent shotgun shell	Weeds	
Plastic bag	Horse turds	FREE!		UFO or aliens
Film crew making shitty indie movie	Yourself		Used condom	
	Graffiti	Teen girl frightened for no apparent reason	Any article of clothing	Fast food wrapper

FOREST BINGO
CARD #2

	Your friend (y'know, the one you're in the forest with)		Pussy willow	Bigfoot
Tick		Wounded hunter	Bag of pills	
	Creepy nature photographer	FREE!	A hobo, complete with one of those cool knapsacks on a stick	Soggy copy of *Swank*
Couple making out	Deer crap	Mud		Guy with a chainsaw, w/ or w/o a hockey mask
Horny, the Living Dead Unicorn		Any Kardashian	Bottle of Boone's Farm	

H-h-hey! I'm a square in F-f-forest Bingo?? Th-that makes me offfffficially f-famous!

I think we could stand to converse about this further...

DR. JEAN-PAUL DOOFUS, PHILOSOPHER

THIS ISSUE'S TOPIC: **BEING AND NUTTINESS**

Good afternoon, students. Dr. J-P. D. here.

Last time we met, we discussed the concept of the "thing-in-itself," and I believe we got in a good three to four minutes of top-notch dialogue before you decided to go make root beer floats instead.

For future reference, I'd like to offer you my thoughts on several pertinent talking points that were made prior to the refreshments:

⊙ The Transition, while considered a state of being, is simultaneously of a nature that is inherently "that which cannot be described," much the same way that one tries to imagine what an entire Rachael Ray TV Network would be like. At the same time, to overly focus on that which "is" can eventually lead to sulking, and even Kant couldn't deal with that.

⊙ The experiential channel of time/space that flows between life and post-life is different for each individual who crosses into and through it. For some, it will be a journey down the Ganges, followed by an illuminating golden walk with the Masters as you prepare for eternal peace and release into the Great Ether. For others, not so much.

⊙ I don't care what your stance on existence is, *My Super Sweet 16* is a sign of the end of days.

⊙ "Post-lifer," "Horde"—these are merely two names given to fleshy units that may or may not attempt to intersect with you in what I call your "circle of reference." The practice of naming objects in such a manner can indeed be profoundly detrimental to the perception of those very same objects. In the end, it may be preferable to, instead, frequently point and loudly say, "That thing" and "That thing" and "That thing."

You know, I may have written "Hell is other people" but I didn't mean it about you. Good health to you and yours and let's experience each other again soon. *Au revoir.*

WHERE THE *K* DID THE *CONSONANTS* GO???

Theme: Remaining Cities in Amer-I-CAN

Below, you'll find a list of cities that still have their vowels in place. But someone swiped the consonants. Hope your post-Disaster *and* post-downsizing geography skills are up to speed because it's up to *you* to fill in the blanks!

Answers on page 103.

1. _ A _ _ A _ I _ _ O

2. _ O U _ _ A _ _ A _/
    _ _ . _ O _ _ _ _ _ I _

3. _ O _ A _ _ I E _ O

4. _ I _ _ _ Y _ _ E _ _ _ I A

5. _ _ O E _ I _ O _

6. _ _ E _ E _ A _ _

7. O _ _ A _ _ E _ _ A _ E

8. _ A _ I _ _ I _ _ E

9. O _ A _ A/
    _ O U _ _ I _ _ U _ _ Y

10. _ I _ _ E
    _ O _ _ _ A _ O _ A
    _ I _ Y

HOW 'BOUT THAT HORDE?

(Interviews with real Horde members and their families by David P. Murphy,
conducted in front of a live studio audience.)

Murphy: (*Audience applause.*) Good day to you. Today we've got Angela McCoy with us, a formerly promising student who, while jogging on her college campus during her junior year, was bitten by a free-ranger. I need to assure all of our readers and those in the studio audience that Angela has been restrained and heavily tranqued, so you have no reason to worry. Along with Angela, her mom, dad, and her 14-year-old sister, Jill, are joining us. Welcome to all of you.

Group: Thank you. (*Angela moans.*)

Murphy: So Mom and Dad McCoy, how long has it been since you've seen Angela?

Mom: Well, since she didn't make the cut to get into Scarlet Shores, our contact has been severely limited. We're allowed to wave to her from an observation platform at the Containment Zone, but this is the closest we've been to her since the Paraguard took her away. Hi, honey.

Angela: Grrrrrrrrrrrrrrrrrrr.

Dad: Don't talk to your mother in that tone, young lady!

Mom: Jim, please!

Jill: How come *she* gets to growl? I *never* get to growl!

Murphy: Hey folks, how 'bout we dial it back a bit? (*Audience titters.*) Angela, I understand you're residing in the CouncilTucky Containment Zone. Is there anything you'd like to tell us about the conditions there?

Angela: (*Hissing at first, then in a distant tone*) Darrrrrrrk. Colllllllld. Beautiful hunger.

Murphy: Well, that doesn't sound particularly pleasant. I thought the 'Tucky had cleaned up its act! (*Audience laughter.*) But, Angela, if you're hungry, we've got donuts and pastries over at the crafts table. Jill, honey, would you mind getting your sister a donut or two?

Jill: No way. And don't call me "honey."

Dad: Jill, do what he asked you to do.

Jill: (*Getting up and storming toward the crafts table*) She *always* gets *everything*! *And* she's a *zombie* now—what *don't* you people understand? She's *not Angela anymore*!

Mom: Jill, please!

Murphy: So go on, Angela—anything else you can tell our viewers and readers? Quite a few of 'em need all the encouragement they can get.

Angela: Darrrrrrk. So very cold. The shriek that will not emerge.

Murphy: Anj, you're losin' me, babe. You been hittin' the Ferlinghetti or what? (*Audience laughter.*)

(*Jill approaches Angela with two donuts as Angela violently lunges at her sister, but is held in place by the cage. Jill throws the donuts at Angela.*)

Jill: Did you see that? She's *always* hated me!

Dad: Angela, that is *not* how you treat your sister!

Mom: Both of you, please!

Angela: (*Devouring the donuts, she pauses and is suddenly much calmer and coherent.*) We will rise. The Great Pushback will fail. And you—you *all* will die. (*Audience ooooohs and then giggles.*)

Mom: Honey, I don't think that's the most upbeat approach to your problems. You were raised better than that.

Dad: Your mom and I expect more from you, missy!

Angela: (*Staring straight into the camera*) You all—will—die. (*Audience laughter.*)

Murphy: (*Clearing his throat to break the moment*) Well, look at the clock! Where the heck does the time go? I'd like to thank Angela and the rest of the McCoy family for sharing their unusual story with us today. Let's hope they're able to resolve their issues before it's too late. Enjoy the rest of the book and I hope to see *you* back here soon. (*Audience applause.*)

The HOOK-Up! —advice from Jane Sheffield,

founder and director of Stiff Competition, the first dating service for someone like YOU!

Q: *Why do women always seem to go for the bad boys? I'm kind, courteous, well mannered, and still have all of my face. Yet, I'm beginning to get the impression that my girl is more interested in a disgustingly coarse and decomposing ruffian. What gives? D.*

Jane: Well, D., perhaps she's simply not the girl for *you*. At Stiff Competition, we're literally overrun with women who are looking for a stand-up guy. They're tired of the general crudeness and constant acting out, and many say they'd be grateful to find a fella with whom they could have an intelligent chat or at least a little peace and quiet. You seem like a reasonably coherent male. Perhaps you should give our 3-month intro package a try. I'll go out on a limb (one of my own, thanks) and say that, if you do, you *won't* regret it.

Q: *I recently discovered that my husband has been using your service as a way to meet and score with post-lifer women. I am sickened and appalled at his behavior. I've taken six showers in a row and still can't get his stench off of me. Honestly, by now I'm disgusted with him and your service. What are you going to do about this and aren't there regulations prohibiting such revolting fraternization? J. (entirety of name withheld, but it DOES end in "Meep.")*

Jane: Sadly, many human men are attracted to the typical post-life female behavioral type: equal parts docile and slutty. I'm sorry your husband is one of those, but please know this: we can't police all of our members. Much of what we do here at S.C. is based on the honor system. We don't have the resources needed to weed out every freak. But what I *can* do for you is have you privately IM me and I'll have his account suspended. And sorry, there are currently no regulations on the books restricting activities such as your husband's. Last month there was an attempt to get one passed through the current session of Congress, but a *certain senator* blocked its passage. Perhaps you *know* him? If so, I recommend you give *him* a piece of your mind. Good luck.

Keep those emails coming, folks. Until we hook-up again—Jane

Thursday evening <u>is</u> *PRIME TIME* on **THE SHORES SHOPPING NETWORK**:

- ⊙ **7–8 p.m.** *The Correcto Comfort Hour.* The weekly gala continues with your hostess, Doris, at the helm. Correcto Fashion Footwear, known for its style and helpful "Footfoam" feature, available for a full sixty minutes at almost reasonable prices!
- ⊙ **8–9 p.m.** *Omaha Trundle Steak-tacular.* Hungry? You *will* be after this savory show. All your favorite cuts in one place and, with our Trundle-To-Your-Door delivery system, your post-life just got tastier!
- ⊙ **9–10 p.m.** *The Summertime Ladies' Collection from The Tacky Factory™.* Our unpredictable friend Jeannie Bison is back with what *may be* her weirdest assortment of garish women's fashions yet! Is she *serious* with this junk? Who can tell—she's got a towel wrapped around her head! And who can understand what the hell she's saying? Dubious clothes but great TV!

I've stayed outta the fray for long enough. Time to sit your butt down and take a look at these shapes and symbols. And stop asking questions, if you know what's good for you!

SHAPES 'N SYMBOLS 'N STUFF!!

Being able to recognize these shapes and symbols could prove to be of real value in your coming days. Draw a line from the object to the correct definition.

SYMBOL	WHAT IT MEANS
▼	Am-Scray! Turn around NOW—this is NOT an exit. Don't make us call the Paraguard.
⬭	Blissium dispensary
↰	First-aid kiosk (probably not staffed)
☺	No Dying Zone
⚡	Muffin Crossing
⬠	Yield to Shufflecraft
▷	Can of refreshing QualiCola or fear-gas cylinder
✚	Defibulator station

You *know* you need
more protein.
And you know how hard it can be to
keep that rack of lamb fresh when you're
constantly on the go.
So why don't you know about

KOOL KLUTCH?

With KOOL KLUTCH,
your meat goes with you!

KOOL KLUTCH—

the world's first refrigerated purse for
women *and* men!

Determine which "flavor" of the Klutch is right for you
—**Bologna, Roast,** or **Whole Pig.**
Or try *all three*!

I'm "chillin'" with
my KOOL KLUTCH. It's
the shiz, bitchez!

The Amazing Maze

Olly olly oxen ackkkff!

It seems Doofus has lost his lunch.
No, he didn't hurl, silly—
he simply misplaced his meal!
See if you can find it for him.

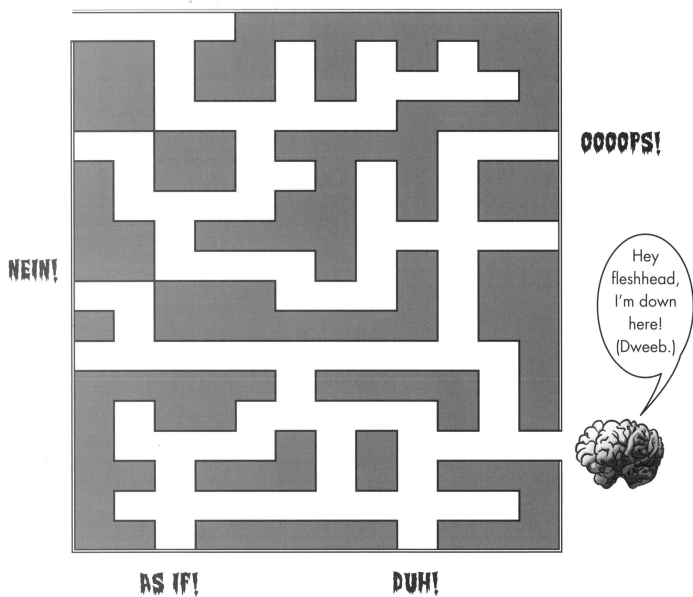

OOOOPS!

NEIN!

Hey fleshhead, I'm down here! (Dweeb.)

AS IF!   DUH!

THE MYSTIC OMAR DOOFUS REVEALS TO YOU:

I see your future, I see France!

YOUR MONTHLY HORDE-OSCOPE

Good gravy, your stars sure have shifted! As a result of the Transition, your birthday has been replaced by what's now called your "biteday." Because of this change, an entirely different and, may we say, far more *accessible* set of zzzodiac signs now apply. Let's take a look at what Omar Doofus sees in the starz for **YOU!**

Harry,
The Ramrod
Mar 21–Apr 20

The way of the aggressive 'Rod takes you on a circuitous path this month, from pushing around punks down by the pier to blowing away a purse snatcher 'cause it feels so right. Your day *will* be made when you're acquitted for poppin' a cap in that drug-smuggling granny. Steer clear of car chases in Russian Hill and, whatever you do, keep out of Daly City.

Morris,
The Bullshit Salesman
Apr 21–May 20

Mighty Morris, you're on a roll and the crowd appears to be buying whatever the hell you're selling. Keep dazzling 'em with classic double-talk and gibberish! Look for a lucrative breakthrough in the next two weeks that will involve mail fraud with a guy in Nigeria. Remember that clients will always be impressed by matching shoes.

Jiminy,
A Cricket
(But Not That One)
May 21–Jun 20

As the moon enters its final quarter and decides to "rest its starters," the enigmatic Cricket will find that post-life is offering him more opportunities than he knows what to do with. Field trips, blind dates, triage, fixins! Let the good times roll, fair Cricket. Keep your distance from salamanders and marionettes. Rub your legs together whenever possible.

Prancer,
Some Reindeer
Jun 21–Jul 21

For a fictional critter, your post-life sure is getting real. Every dream you've dreamed is aligning itself in the ether and will arrive soon, except for those being delivered by UPS. Even the promotion you'd thought impossible will be bumped into the way better "snowball's chance" category. A romance with a Virginia is a strong possibility. Beware of Shriners selling door-to-door steaks.

**Leona,
That Pharmacist Gal
Jul 22–Aug 21**

**Virginia,
The "Virgin"
Aug 22–Sep 21**

When the chips are down, everyone always comes to you, don't they? You're eternally willing to dispense advice as needed or whatever else you can offer. Dear Leonas: with Saturn entering the House of Pies in the following four weeks, you'll notice a new wrinkle to your situation regarding an overweight chemist acquaintance. Do not give behind-the-counter cold remedies to people with mullets. And keep in mind that, in the big picture, there is no mortar without a pestle.

Ginnys are known for being a forceful sign, capable of great willpower. Additionally, they're famous for their persuasive skills, like how they're able to get men to buy them booze at all hours. Soon these attributes will come in handy as circumstances regarding the Winter Formal will require attention (and could involve some knee-capping). One of your friends will attempt to make the case that even intercourse isn't technically "sex." Ginnys: shy away from men who look like they're posing for JC Penney ads.

**Barbra,
The Scales
Sep 22–Oct 22**

**Scooter,
The Bitey Dog
Oct 23–Nov 21**

You who are born under this 9' Bosendorfer-shaped constellation are constantly creative, particularly this month. Keep your ears open for a multi-level marketing opportunity that includes karaoke. If you get a chance to sing a duet, take it! Avoid pentatonic individuals—their self-limiting nature can be exhausting for you. Unrelated "note": No direct sunlight for you unless your Hazmat gown is back from the cleaners.

Who's a good sign? Scooters are a lively and lusty breed, and these next thirty days are all about chasing your ambitions or at least a squirrel. Don't let the post-life pass you by—get out there, grab it by the leg, and shake it 'til its neck is broken. Time will tell if that recent love interest is really the one or simply a place to bury a bone. Sit.

Dontravius,
The White Attendant with a
Black Man's Name
Nov 22–Dec 20

A huge change is coming for the Attendants and it begins now! Your worries are laid to rest, especially your anxiety about the fact that you resemble *no one* in your family. The future has something grand planned for you, so RSVP as soon as you're contacted. No need to enclose a SASE—that would be seem pushy. Avoid cleaning shotguns.

Cappy,
The Disturbing Old Goat
Dec 21–Jan 19

Lately, you're having a harder time getting people to listen to you. Maybe if you weren't so weird and creepy, Cappies, folks would be more inclined to tolerate your lectures regarding the superiority of the steam engine and why Millard Fillmore was our finest president. Why not lay off the spontaneous outbursts of laughter; they're bugging everyone. And consider Romerin.

Aquariums,
Pretty Water Thingees
Jan 20–Feb 18

The saltwater sign of the zzzodiac will experience even more humidity in the coming days, and that's good news! Love abounds for Aquariums and there's no stopping you now. Buy a better deodorant and come out of that little castle of yours. While you're exploring your steamy surroundings, keep away from the "bottom feeder" types. Wetter is better and your entire sign is about to get soaked! Have a towel handy and enjoy the swim. Stock up on TetraMin.

Feces,
The Turd
Feb 19–Mar 20

Yet another troubled month is coming for the beleaguered Feces. Money problems worsen and, if you have children, they're gonna be a handful. Additionally, your mate may be surly, you should keep your pets indoors, and don't get on any planes. This current crummy streak is due to the constellation Skippy, which continues to crumble in the northern sky, as it has for the last 47 months. Oh yeah, one more thing: get a checkup—there's something nasty in your large intestine.

Premiering next month on—

BABY, IT'S DEAD OUTSIDE: THE SERIES

Veteran private eye Jack Crank works the graveyard shift in the seediest part of post-Disaster Pittsyldelphia. Join him as he explores the even-darker underbelly of the Megacity of Brotherly Steel. Thursdays at 9 p.m. EST. *(Mature content and graphic dining scenes—viewer discretion is advised.)*

YOUR NUMBER'S UP!!

So you know, 6 through 8 are causing me major swelling!

This'll give you a head cramp! Figure out the next logical number in the sequences below.

Answers on page 103.

1.	3 7 12 18 25 ?	_____
2.	9 5 10 6 11 ?	_____
3.	2 4 8 16 32 ?	_____
4.	-10 -5 0 5 10 ?	_____
5.	100 95 89 82 74 ?	_____
6.	1.3 2.87 7.32 8.776 ?	_____
7.	½ 34.2 ¼ 89.1 2/3 ?	_____
8.	17 19 23 29 π ?	_____

MZ. MANNERZ
"MISTRESS OF THE POLITE"

Dear Readers: I've been getting a number of letters recently asking variations of the same question—how do dating rules differ in the post-life?

I confess that I've got issues about how best to guide y'all. Honestly, I believe this topic deserves a two-pronged response. First, the answer that I wish was true: there *should be no difference*. The proper progression for developing intimacy within an evolving, romantic relationship should mimic the same stages in your former life. Having said that, the other half of my response unfortunately represents the reality—you people are *pigs*. I've got news for you—the world is not your oyster or your public love den. Get a clue. Keep your amorous activities limited to your residences and *not* in ShuffleCrafts or in the "Housewares" aisles of QualiKo. Additionally, y'all *really* need to pare back on those pharmaceuticals you're taking that are putting your libidos into overdrive and screwing up your boundaries. Just as in your prior life, romance is best when the shades are drawn and the lights are out.

Mz. Mannerz can be reached at mannerz@mzmannerz.com. But please, don't send photos.

WERD SURCH 3

Again with the hidden werdz?

Answers on page 104.

```
B  A  W  B  W  P  A  I  N
R  O  W  I  E  U  K  Y  E
O  R  D  T  S  T  A  B  E
A  T  I  Y  C  R  O  A  K
C  A  R  O  T  I  D  Y  A
L  L  T  R  A  S  T  W  P
O  F  N  B  A  Y  H  V  U
T  E  A  G  E  S  U  W  T
S  V  P  W  E  T  D  O  N
C  E  J  O  E  E  A  U  P
R  R  T  N  K  M  P  N  U
E  Y  E  B  A  L  L  D  K
A  T  H  O  R  A  X  E  E
M  C  R  U  S  H  E  D  W
```

Can YOU find these hidden werdz?

CROAK	AORTA	CAROTID	KAPUT
PUTRISYSTEM	CLOTS	DIRTNAP	OWIE
THORAX	TOES	TANK	WOUNDED
BETA	EYEBALL	SCREAM	FEVER
PAIN	CRUSHED	PUKE	GAS
THUD	BIT	STAB	EEEK
BRO	BODY	EEK	AXE

(Please remember: there's a BIG difference between "Eek" and "Eeek.")

Somebody, and it sooo *wasn't me,* messed up my toys! Please help me out by crossing out the one below that's different from the others. And if you see that damn Doofus, do me a favor—tell him when I get a hold of him, he's dead.

Celebrity Spotlight

GET THE LATEST BUZZ!

Local hottie, **Doris**, was recently seen out on the town at our very own Shores, dining with her latest paramour at the freshly refurbished Gristle's Steakhaus. She seemed to enjoy herself as she guzzled six Cosmos while pushing around food on her plate. Meanwhile, her famous icon-of-an-ex, **Diligent**, who happens to be staying at the Shores during his *Z4Z* book tour, is not exactly brooding while Doris flits about. He was spotted with three—count 'em, three—different lifers last week at Club Tibia.

Dateline QCasino: A man calling himself "**Dr. Doofus**" won the coveted "Buffet Customer of the Year Award" during a special event held last month. Music was provided by the Guy Mutch Trio and special guest Sen. Frederick Meep was on hand to present a plaque and an oversized edible check to the ravenous winner. Sadly, Dr. Doofus became so frisky that he got into a scuffle with the runners-up and had to be forcibly removed from the premises. Despite the bizarre ending to the evening, our hearty congrats go out to the good doctor!

Post-Lifer **Manny Cottonball**, the oldest living resident at Scarlet Shores Beta, celebrated his 43rd birthday last week at a gala party thrown by the staff. Punch was served and a dead time was had by all. Manny got his birthday wish: his last name was legally changed to "Cottonball." No more nicknames for Manny—happy birthday, Manny, or should I say "Mr. Cottonball!"

Drunken Doris Update: **Doris** has been witnessed at Gristle's After Dark, where she appeared profoundly intoxicated. Our sources tell us that she was popping Blissiums like tic tacs and ended up making out with a female bartender. Is this the beginning of another downhill skid for Doris?

It looks like that loveable corporate heavy, **Chomps the Clown**, is at it again. As he was coming out of a trendy Burbank eatery, Chomps went after the pitiable paparazzi who were wooing him for a pic. Allegedly, he put all three photogs in the hospital. Lawsuits *or* disappearances are sure to follow. Oh, Chomps!

Friend to all post-living creatures, **Dr. Kenneth Beaker**, was honored last weekend by the QualiCorps Humanitarian Foundation for his years of tireless service on behalf of the post-lifer community and his work involving the teaching of ballet to chimps. Dr. Beaker was presented with a medal from the President's Council on Fitness and Eclairs (a medal personally autographed by **Pres. Dutch Bingo**, might I add). Dr. Beaker's latest wife, **Rebecca**, was on his arm and looked dazzling in her fiery Ralph Q gown.

Final Doris update: In a stunning turn of events. **Diligent** was spotted earlier, rushing into Gristle's After Dark, and whisking the still-staggering, shit-faced **Doris** out the door and into a waiting ShuffLimo. Details to follow as soon as they're available!

SUBSTITUTION FRENZY!!

Answers unavailable at time of printing.

Change only one letter in each word
to arrive at the word at the bottom!
(*Warning: these will be demanding.*)

H-hey, I'm no
M-M-MENSA m-member,
but s-something's
s-s-screwy here!

We'll start off easy, ok?

```
D O G
D _ G
B I G
```

Not so hard, huh? Try this one on for size!

```
P A I N
_ _ _ N
_ _ _ N
T R O W E L
```

This baby is even more difficult. Have at thee, wordly knave!

```
S W I S H
_ _ _ _ H
_ _ Ø _ _
_ Ñ _ _ _ _
_ _ _ Æ _ _
_ Ÿ _ _ _ _
S Q U I D
```

So, howdja do?

That's a shame. Well, no need to get
snippy about it. I mean, it's only a
puzzle. It's not like it defines your
intelligence or anyth—oops.

No Inactivity Book would be complete without some form of the world's numero-uno numbers game, Sudoku (which, you'll remember, is not at all like "Sodoku," which is a deadly disease you can get from rats and is nowhere near as fun as these puzzles).

Anyway, we've adapted the game a bit for your comfort level and think you'll find this version to be to your liking. No more blinding pain from basic math—simply figure out what number is missing. What could be easier? And easier *is* better!

Answers on page 104.

Let's play—

ZUDOKU!

This is kind of a letdown, Dave.

8	4	7
?	1	6
2	9	3

Difficulty Rating: (negative ★ ★)

Yeah, well, what good is a puzzle if you can't solve it, I say!

1	2	3
4	5	6
7	8	?

Difficulty Rating: (negative ★ ★ ★)

LETTERS TO MACK—
THE PSYCHOTIC NEIGHBORHOOD BUTCHER

Note #1: *Dear Mack: I frequently shop at your store, but recently I've noticed a change in the quality of your meats. Did I just get a "bum roast" or is something different? Thanks. —Ira*

MACK: Yeah, Ira, I know who you are—you're that hypnotist guy. We've said hi before and, believe you me, I've appreciated your business over the years. That being said, if you ever infer anything untoward regarding my products again, I swear to God, I'll have you dumped in a Containment Zone so quickly your dumb head will spin. Let's see you hypnotize your way outta that, ya putz!! Did I answer your question?

Note #2: *Dear Mack: Last week, in a hurry, I grabbed an item from the Clearance Freezer, stuck it in my fridge, and then popped it into the oven last night. According to the label, it's something called a "Trundle Roast." While it was quite delicious at the time, it had an unusual texture and left a very salty and unpleasant aftertaste in my family's mouths. May I ask where this "Trundle" comes from, please? —Mrs. Dr. B. Linky*

MACK: No, Mrs. Linky, you may not.

Note #3: *Dear Mack: I've found some of your recent replies to your fan letters to be less than helpful. My friend, Ira, the hypnotist, wrote to you not long ago and, in your response, you were downright rude. Additionally, I've noticed you leering at the ladies, and my wife in particular, while you're pretending to work behind the meat case. It's unprofessional and tacky. It seems like ever since you changed suppliers, you've been an entirely different guy. Whatever happened to the "Good Old Mack" we knew and with whom we used to kid? Where did that happy-go-lucky guy go? —Dean*

MACK: I'll tell ya what happened to "Good Old Mack"—he got strong-armed by the freakin' thugs at QualiCorps Meats into either a) signing up exclusively with their distribution system and their scary crap or b) spending a night in a motel room with Chomps the Clown. Forgive me, but I caved like a San Fernando sinkhole. As for the rest of it, Dean, you're a cretin and, if you know what's good for you, you'll stop asking questions. I'm sure Chomps would love to give you a complimentary session. And by the way, your wife is *hot!*

Hangdude!

Everyone knows how this game is played.
Grab a friend and have that "person" look up the answers while you guess. Neat!
(And I only changed the name cuz the estate of the late Merv Griffin has it out for me.
I'm thinkin' it might have something to do with that unfortunate kaftan gag I once made.)

Answers on page 104.

PUZZLE #1:

NOUNS THAT
SHOULD NEVER HAVE
BEEN MERGED

_ _ _ _   _ _ _ _ _ _

_ _ _ _ _   _ _ _ _ _

PUZZLE #2:

ADORABLE
DEAD PAL

_ _ _ _ _ _,   _ _ _   _ _ _ _ _ _

_ _ _ _   _ _ _ _ _ _ _

PUZZLE #3:

CLASSIC POST-DISASTER
TV SHOW

_ _ _   _ _ _ _ _ _ _ _ _ _

_ _ _ _ _ _ _/_ _ _ _ _ _ _ _

_ _ _ _

TWINZ!!

Here's a little something left over from Diligent's Photoshop Phinal.

Two of these images are identical. Can **YOU** find them?

Diligent
+
Doris

DOOFUS
+
Boris

Diligent
+
Florist

Diligent
+
Doofus

INDIGENT
+
Morris

MEEP
+
WHOMEV

Diligent
+
Doris

DUTCH
+
DORIS

KONSTITUTIONAL KORNER
with Catherine Goldman, Esq.
whereby said "clients" seek free legal advice from a colossal bee-yatch

Ms. Goldman: The election is looming in a few months and I feel very strongly about getting our dopey president, President Dutch Bingo, out of that office and kicked to the curb. I am new to the Shores but am now being told I won't be allowed to cast my vote. Can you help me? *Bonnie*

Catherine Goldman, Esq.: No, I can't help you. You don't get to vote anymore. A clause in The Post-Lifer Rights Re-revision and Bacon Standards Act took care of that little detail. Sucks to be you, Bonnie. And by the way, I'm voting for Bingo. Boo-yah!

Dear Cathy: The other day I received a notice in the mail concerning the liquidation of a home I own in Sacracisco. There is no phone number on the letter or a return address. How can this be? And how can I fight this? *Rex*

Catherine Goldman, Esq.: Who the hell do you think you are, Rex? I don't know you; don't ever call me "Cathy." My mother calls me Cathy and I hate it! Now, to answer your question: you're screwed. Section 8.3.a of The Post-Lifer Rights Re-revision and Bacon Standards Act clearly forbids you from owning any property in the post-life. Hope you took pics of the place. Oh yeah, and expect a bill—that's two questions.

Direct all correspondence to ibillu@goldmanlaw.com
Clients with more than one question will be billed. No exceptions.

CROZZWERDZ 2

Yet another Phil Shortz original.
(See, he's not *that* crappy.)

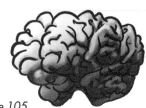

I'm beggin' ya, not this hellhole of a puzzle again! Nooooooo...

Answers on page 105.

ACROSS

Wacky futuristic S. Connery film (6)

Don't have a _____ attack (4)

At this point, you'd feel lucky to have this skin disease (6)

Likewise with this teenage dermal eruption (3)

Goofy Russian spacecraft (5)

Old axe-shaped weapon that would hert yer hed (sounds like "commercials" synonym) (3)

Nose nickname esp. for those Mediterranean types (7)

Demolished, like that farm house (5)

Really dumb spelling of Papa's name from Dead Bear Family (5)

DOWN

_____ and confused like you (5)

A few of your personalities believe you might be _____ (6)

Like that maze on page 72 (7)

Worries or what a P-lifer does while waiting for the CareBox to arrive (8)

Section of a dumb song (6)

If a Paraguard zigs, then the Horde guy _____ (4)

Male hybrid of a yak. Really. (3)

Slang for unproductive lout or _____ around the house (4)

____ and herz (3)

THE EVEN DEADLIER BLOCKS!

Take the letters in the word "TIE" and—oh, please, I'm absolutely *not* going through this explanation again. Go back to page 20 if you need help.

Answers on page 105.

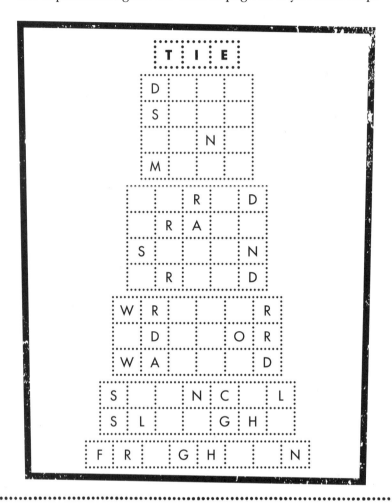

RIDDLEZ!!

Why did the Horde member cross the road?

      To kill something on the other side.

      And then pull it apart and eat it. Grody! —*Chrissy, Age 9*

What made Doofus put on a banana suit?

      He thought it would give him more "a peel." —*Timmy, Age 8*

Why did Cheezy, the dead bear cub, fail his spelling test?

      He was afraid of B's. —*Jacob, Age 32*

What's the difference between the "very best thing ever that I enjoy so much" and cottonballs?

      Nothing! —*Manny, Age 43*

88   ZOMBIES FOR ZOMBIES: THE PLAY & WERK BUK

Next time you're in Port-Au-Prince
make sure you stop by the city's most prestigious school—

THE PORT-AU-PRINCE CAPON ACADEMY

with the stunning new
Pat Robertson Wing
rebuilt and ready to go!

Come by, have lunch, and see the beautiful new wing that's been added to our school, funded by the abundant guilt of *Mr. Pat Robertson.*

When visiting, talk to any of our on-campus counselors to learn how EZ it can be for YOU to receive the most coveted advanced degree of all—the PhZ.

Tour our grounds. Check out the dorms. Pet the goats. Meet *Pat Robertson.*

Your education begins as soon as you sign the contract. And submit to the mandatory admission "ritual."

THE PORT-AU-PRINCE CAPON ACADEMY

"Shaping Lives and Post-Lives Alike."

I WONDER...

Dear Werk Buk: I wonder how these Scarlet Shores facilities get built so quickly. *Tammy, Sacracisco*

Tammy, when an area is targeted to receive a glistening, modern Scarlet Shores facility, the cue is given to thousands of workers at all four of our gargantuan assembly plants to once more begin the monumental process. At each plant, different teams work together to assemble large sections of the facility. One plant may construct the living quarters, another the medical areas, another the Hall of Fixins, and so on. This is done so that, by the time the sections arrive at the building site, they're ready to be joined together like a massive jigsaw puzzle where all the pieces mostly fit except, as usual, for the few crucial sections that were manufactured by those dipshits at the Orlanderdale plant. Those noobs couldn't follow a blueprint at gunpoint and I gotta believe that their foreman's dyslexic. Anyway, this kind of cooperative approach ensures consistent construction techniques and the best quality control ever devised in the last few years. So, the next time you see huge chunks of structures being moved on a flatbed or a barge, take comfort in the fact that a new Scarlet Shores facility is working its way to a community in need.

I WONDER...   **89**

Wanna know why I'm so pissed off all the time? Well, here's one of those lousy origin stories like they have in the funny books that'll explain it to ya. Sound good? Yeah—I hope you choke on it!

SCARLET STORIEZ 4:

CHOMPS GETS A ROOM

Chomps had memories of being a pleasant enough person once upon a time, but those memories were rapidly eroding. He could recall that he *had* been a competent, good-natured clown at one time. He'd made children giggle, pleased parents, and all that other happy horse hockey. But the cheerfulness, and his other finer traits, began to exit the arena once he got bit.

Chomps had been hired for a birthday party back when he was known as "Sparky," because he was doing more of a fireman-based theme then. He remembered working the room that day, performing the usual gags with balloons and seltzer. The carpet midgets were eating it up, which was the whole point. He'd glanced at his watch and realized he only had a few minutes left on the gig. Then he'd get the hell out of Dodge, track down the nearest nondescript bar, and try to catch the end of the Jets game.

As he was finishing up the act, he looked up from his watch and saw an odd, pale child walking toward him, holding out a paper plate full of shitty-looking sheet cake. As Chomps nodded to the kid in appreciation and reached out to take the plate, the brat (P1V1 infected, it turned out) lunged at him and bit him on the arm. It was all Chomps could do right then and there to not take the kid out.

Anyway, that's how he remembered the moment when everything went haywire and started to head downhill. Now ever since the Transition, his memories seemed to be increasingly colored by a relentless anger. No matter what recollection he reached for, his "red filter of rage" (as he called it) colored its tone and mood.

For the record, Chomps was a special case—the rare post-lifer who didn't respond to the recommended drugs or any of the feel-good crap that was thrown at him after being infected. Rather than becoming increasingly more mellow from the effects of his alleged diminished cranial capacity, powerful pharmaceuticals and dumbass self-help programs, he'd only gotten pissed. Pissed that he'd been bitten. *Really* pissed about that. Pissed about the toll the virus had taken on his appearance. Pissed about the fact that he'd been robbed of half of his speech and motor skills (and yet he could still think relatively clearly). Even pissed about the timing: his life had been peaking in a number of ways. His kids had started liking him again, his ex-wife had been more civil, and he'd just met that new gal, Jane, online. She seemed like a sweetheart and had a great job with the Feds in Nebraska. He would've liked to have met her in his former life, but not now. He was too messed up. Man, he was *really* pissed about that. And, of course, he was pissed about the Jets but, then, he'd always been pissed about the Jets.

So, a few months ago, when four suits from QualiCorps showed up at Chomps' residence at Scarlet Shores Pomona to talk with him about his "anger issues," he found it strange. Why the hell would these QualiCorps guys care about me, he wondered, and how would they even know about my clown career?

Chomps was aware that his stay at the Shores was already on thin ice, being endangered on a regular basis by his bad attitude and the fact that, when startled, he hissed like the Horde. He was frequently told how lucky he was to be a resident there, but he didn't feel lucky and he'd never liked Pomona. Additionally, he was tired of being reminded about the gratitude he was supposed to feel. "Glass half full, my ass," he often mumbled.

After another interview with the suits, Chomps was offered a deal: an opportunity to put his terrible temper to good use. They reasoned that clowns made most everyone uncomfortable and, if a company was to have an angry, Horde-ish clown in their back pocket as a way to resolve certain situations, it could be beneficial for everyone concerned. The suits also stipulated that such attempts at resolution might occasionally call for "lite" violence and intimidation tactics, and they asked him directly if Chomps would be fine with that. Chomps remembered nodding and mouthing, "No problem."

Finally, the suits—a Mr. Gold in particular—expressed enthusiasm about Chomps joining the group and voiced their appreciation for the kind of rare creature he was becoming. Gold actually circled him at one point, as if Chomps was a recently purchased pedigreed racehorse. "You're everything good about the virus," Mr. Gold had said, beaming as he shook Chomps' hand. Chomps had never heard a sentence quite like that before and, mostly, it pissed him off because there was *nothing* good about the virus. But, he did have to admit he liked Gold's strange admiration and the perks Gold was offering. Chomps would do right by this guy.

Not long after, Chomps was removed from the Pomona facility and placed in a new residence, in an area of Burbank that was still relatively safe. His pad was a full one-bedroom apartment (which felt luxurious to Chomps) with a perpetually stocked fridge and bar, and, best of all, an immense Super Hi-Def television with every global sports channel available, courtesy of QualiCorps. The company had placed him there because of the apartment's proximity to The Sleep-ee Time Travel Motel. The suits had bought The Sleep-ee Time a couple years ago for a number of specific reasons—for part-time housing, all manner of client entertainment, storage, and for a use known only to a few: Chomps' persuasion sessions.

The suits had a brilliant vision. Chomps was allowed to become exactly who he wanted to be now, which was everything he'd never been before: a thug, a prick, a nightmare, a heavy, a terror, the last resort, that guy you *don't* want to meet in a dark alley, the bogeyman. He was the embodiment of everything that could go wildly wrong in a moment.

The sessions were simple. Chomps would get a call at any given time and be instructed to arrive at The Sleep-ee Time within the hour. Then Chomps would put on his suit, inflate the balloons, fill his satchel with tools of his own dark invention, and head over to Room 209. It was the one in the corner, with no unit above and only a dumpster below. Once there, he would set up shop and relax until the knock at the door. Then, two or three lackeys would escort an unknown, pathetic, struggling schmuck in through the door and, usually, as soon as the schmuck saw Chomps sitting in the dimly lit room, holding the balloons and glaring at him, that was all the persuasion the schmuck needed.

It happened that there was something so unnerving about putting a person in a room with a living dead clown, that most sessions lasted mere minutes. Chomps would then wait while the lackeys loaded the schmuck back into the car and, shortly thereafter, Chomps would be back home on the couch, yelling at a Jets game.

He'd learned that one doesn't need much in the way of speech or motor skills to be intimidating—the secret was in the setup and just how horrifying you made it.

This is not to say that Chomps found the sessions where little effort was expended to be particularly satisfying. He far preferred the ones where he was challenged by the occasional hard-ass who refused to be frightened. In those circumstances, Chomps got to break out his tools. *Those* were the precious moments, when Chomps had the chance to flex his anger like a muscle in his soul that ached to be stretched. And, as always, once the red filter of rage arrived on the scene, the rest was poetry.

His best work to date was the night he spent with a local butcher who didn't want to embrace a new distribution system the suits had offered. This guy—Mack—didn't bat an eyelash when the lackeys brought him into Room 209. He was remarkably cool at first and even started snickering, which Chomps interpreted as a form of disrespect. As Mack was roughly strapped into a chair and gagged, the snickering stopped. The lackeys moved away from Mack and waited by the doorway.

Chomps stared at Mack dispassionately. He got up and limped over to Mack, never losing eye contact. He untied one of the balloons from its string and began to rub it, making a grating squeaking noise. All that was audible in the room was Chomps' labored breathing, Mack's muffled grunts, and the awful sound Chomps made with the balloon. Chomps felt like a conductor on a podium in front of his own captive symphony.

As Chomps began to fiddle with the nozzle of the balloon, the lackeys took their cue and placed kerchiefs over their mouths. Mack craned his neck to see what their shuffling was about and, upon seeing the kerchiefs, his grunts became cries that reeked of hysteria. Chomps undid the knotted nozzle and held it tightly so that no gas escaped. He then stuck it under Mack's nose, released several bursts and stood back.

Truth was, Chomps had never been told exactly *what* was in the gas tanks that resided in a closet of his apartment, but he'd been told *never* to inhale it. This was why Chomps had designed his red rubber nose to be fitted with miniature nasal filters. He already had issues with breathing; he didn't need any more problems. Chomps figured there had to be helium in the tanks, but had no idea what else was in the mixture.

So, it came as no surprise when Mack started to scream, his eyes bulging from his head like an astronaut in reentry. After a beat, the lackeys closed in, whispered something to Mack, and, upon getting no response, signaled for Chomps to continue.

Mack made it through nearly a half a balloon, the Joyless Buzzer, and the Herty-Squirty tie before he finally broke. As the lackeys led him away, gasping for air and weeping like a Wal-Mart toddler, Chomps was impressed. Mack must've been a big shot in his time, he thought. Oh well, *his* time was over—it was Chomps' time now.

One evening, several weeks later, Chomps was putting the finishing touches on a Double Trundle Burger when the phone rang. He was needed again, but this time would be different—a town car would be by in thirty minutes to pick him up. He was to be in costume and to bring all his gear. This session would not be at The Sleep-ee Time but, instead, he'd be making a house call.

Chomps was pissed about the change of venue and the fact that, without a doubt, he'd miss the kickoff of the Jets game. He was also annoyed about being forced to do his work elsewhere. Room 209 was his canvas, his block of granite, his blank page. Without it, how could he do his job? he wondered. Chomps mumbled "Improvisation," shrugged, and got ready for the job.

When his ride arrived, he got even more pissed. The car was cramped—too many lackeys inside—and, in such close proximity, his balloons were bugging the hell out of him. Additionally, his car mates kept fidgeting and looking away from him. Worst of all, not one of the lackeys could figure out how to work the car's tiny TV. Chomps shook his head; for the first time he wondered if his job might not be everything he thought it was.

When the car came to an abrupt stop, Chomps could see the group had arrived at an underground garage, which sat below a sizeable structure of some sort. Once he stepped out of the vehicle, balloons in one hand, satchel in the other, the lackeys tried to hurry him along, which everyone always did (and that pissed him off, too). Chomps was briskly escorted into the elevator, the "penthouse" button was pushed and, just before the doors closed, the lackeys left.

The elevator stopped, the bell rang and the doors opened to reveal a large and lavish apartment. An entirely different set of lackeys appeared, gestured to Chomps, and wordlessly walked him down a hallway to a bedroom. Chomps' eyes weren't as reliable as they once had been, and, with the drapes drawn, it took several seconds to make out the scene before him.

As it happened, there were a handful of people in the room and several were familiar to Chomps. He didn't feel capable of a reaction resembling astonishment, but something damn close to it momentarily surfaced within him. Three of the original QualiCorps suits were gathered around a guy in a chair, who appeared as if he'd been roughed up. Once Chomps focused, he saw through the guy's bruises and blood that it was Mr. Gold. Suits punishing suits, Chomps thought. What could possibly be next?

It was explained to Chomps that Mr. Gold had broken rank and become a Horde sympathizer. In doing so, he'd passed along vital information to the other sympathizers and the three remaining suits needed to know the extent of the damage. Chomps was asked if he understood what had to happen and, in reply, he gave the three a look that would wither a rose. Setting his satchel down, he raised his right index finger to signal there would be a brief pause. He then shuffled over to the TV, found the Jets game, cranked up the volume, and returned to the group.

Mr. Gold wasn't gagged at this point and attempted to engage Chomps in a low and urgent tone. His words were a sonic blur, but Chomps heard phrases such as "They're lying; this has nothing to do with the Horde," "I understand you," and "Don't do this." As Chomps went for the first balloon, Gold continued to make his point: "For God's sake, listen to me! People are being placed in Containment Zones who aren't infected. They're put there so they'll shut up. It's a way to make them permanently disappear. It's all *crowd control*, Chomps." In reply, Chomps approached Gold, rubbing the balloon, and making that dreadful sound.

As he stared at Gold, Chomps briefly considered walking away from this session. He remembered how well he'd been treated by Gold and, in that instant, felt a strong allegiance to him. But, as the red filter fell into place once more, that allegiance died. A deal was a deal and it was time to go to work.

The roomful of lackeys and suits covered their mouths and noses as Chomps centered the balloon's nozzle under Gold's nose. As the customary screaming crescendoed, Chomps noticed how absent he felt from the proceedings. He glared harder at the writhing figure below him and, as Gold came completely unglued, Chomps was sorry he'd turned up the TV—the Jets' quarterback had gotten sacked for a safety.

QUIZZZTIME!!!: CHOMPS GETS A ROOM

Please circle the correct answers.

For cryin' out loud, just go!: page 105.

1. Chomps is a merry fellow.
   True   False

2. His balloons are magical.
   True   False

3. Jets fans are nuts.
   True   False

4. Mr. Gold shoulda shut his freakin' yap.
   True   False

5. Chomps has anger issues.
   True   False

6. Did you tell Chomps that I said he had anger issues?
   True   False

7. You're a snitch!
   True   False

8. Crap. That's Chomps at my front door, isn't it? I'm so screwed.
   True   False

Helpful Hints From Hermione
The Domestic Engineer of the DAMNED!

Larry Fox:

Hermione, how do I get bloodstains out of silk?

Hermione:

Larry, that's a tough one, but I think I've got your answer. First of all, get yourself a nice cut of Trundle and, as soon as you can, rub that meat-stuff right into the stain. (Whatever Trundle is, it sure has some great uses, doesn't it?) Then, mix together a cup of cold water, a teaspoon of your own saliva (the enzymes will help further break down the blood), a shot of baking soda, a dash of vinegar, and soak the whole garment in that mixture for a day or two. If possible, bury the whole thing in a clay pot for the better part of a week. Let me know if that works.

Debbie Matzu:

Hermione, how do I get bloodstains out of velvet?

Hermione:

Debbie, at first I thought you'd stumped me, but then I recalled a trick my grandmother showed me when I was a kid. Put a medium-sized sauce pan on the stove and heat up the following ingredients: 2 cups water, 3 habaneros, 3 tablespoons of hot sauce, a dash of lighter fluid, and a fig. Let it boil down to a brownish paste and remove it from the stove. Allow the goo to cool, spread the paste on the stain, and light a match to it. [Be sure to shield your eye(s).] Poof—once the smoke clears, you'll see that the stain has cleared as well!

Jimmy (The Gutz) De Luca:

Hermione, how do I get bloodstains out of leather?

Hermione:

You don't.

IT'S TIME TO—

EAT—SOME—CLOCK!!

Feel the burn, Shlomo!

A Great Way to Shave Time Off *Your* Transition *AND* Learn About Your New **Body!**

On average, a human being will shed 40 pounds of skin during a lifetime. *(So be careful with what you've got left. It won't be regrowing now, unless you've got one of those cool Kafka Booths.)*

Men have more blood than women. Men have 1.5 gallons while women have 0.875 gallons. *(Horde members would say the lesson here is to go for the guys.)*

The human brain ceases to grow past the age of 18 *(or whatever age YOU currently are).*

Avoiding your financial problems can make you twice as likely to develop gum disease. *(What's your excuse?)*

The stomach of homo sapiens requires a full hour to digest cow's milk. *(Oddly, it only takes half that time to digest an actual stomach.)*

A human heart beats over 100,000 times a day! *(That number may be a tad lower for you and, by "tad," I mean a buttload.)*

A person's skull is composed of 29 different bones. *(Like a buffet with a neck!)*

It takes 72 different muscles to produce human speech. *(Interestingly, only 42 of those muscles are needed to whimper.)*

Your nose is the same length as your thumb. *(Not anymore.)*

The storage capacity of the human brain exceeds 4 terabytes. *(These days, you're probably lookin' at more like a gig. Basically, you're a JumpDrive.)*

A six-year-old child laughs about 300 times a day. *(See? It's good to be more childlike!)*

In a recent study it was discovered that 25 percent to 33 percent of people exposed to light sneeze *(while a significant number of you may tend to cringe).*

A human thighbone has been proven to be stronger than concrete. *(And sweeter than* **QualiCola***!)*

It has been observed that certain worms will attempt to eat themselves if they get hungry enough. *(Don't even think about it.)*

DelitefulDoris: re #Doofus—might to have to hit that. He's got the bad boy thing going in a big way. Rwrrrrr!

WHO'S TWEEZERING® US RIGHT NOW??!

MCottnbll: I luv ctnblls!

beaker42: goin' batty w/the wiff. may have to score me some hootch.

murphyhost: book seems to be going well. hard to know how it's being received though…

MrsLinky: having brakes checked then off to lunch!

meatymack: damn #clown showed up at the shop again today. might be time for my vacation.

Seafudcapn: WTF is #trundle, anyway?

farnerlad: bajillionth day patrolling #Zone. nothing happens. i really should hug one of 'em for kicks.

dedbeardad: need hunny. thought i saw a hive neerby.

RebeccaB: off for a swim and then brunch!

Meepster: aftr renaming vote im sooooooo gettn trashed w/that redhdd intrn.

scjane: wht's w/guys & pst-lifer women? creepy. and why did the CA clown guy stop writing to me?

doofus: thinkk dorus liks mee. hmmm, who's fer lunch?

1horned1: t-t-tell assistant t-to resched #portlandia reading & rrrrreplenish s-s-sugar jar

timmy66: #zombie walk = coolest thing ever!

yrprezprezdb: this is a secure line, right?

Kandylip: time for a workout and then meet Kenny for lunch!

diligentgent: uhhh, #doris and #DOOFUS??!! why??

Comings AND Goings

Obituaries

Dean Wright, 41, founder and owner of the ShuffLimo company, was killed by a falling anvil outside of Mack's House of Meats. Dean is survived by his wife, Louise, and his twin sons, Maury and Connie. Services to be announced.

Mrs. Dolores Linky, 52, of brake failure on Hwy. 12. Dolly's charity work speaks for itself or could if she wasn't so darned deceased. Dr. Bernard Linky, her loving husband, would like to thank everyone for the numerous cards and cutlets. There will be a private service for family only.

Manny Cottonball, 43, of old age. A good sport if ever there was one, Manny was one of the earliest "infectees" of P1V1. What's remarkable, though, is that Manny was born with antibodies that prevented the virus from doing the profound damage it did to others. Consequently, Manny's blood has been used to make several anti-viral drugs; in this way, he will live on. Services at S.S. Beta, followed by cotton candy, cake, and Twister.

Ira Owens, 39, found deceased in a Containment Zone. Investigation continues. Ira was known for his warmth and humility and his sucky hypnotism act. He will be sorely missed by all, but especially by his corgi, Kreskin. Memorial at The Little Castle by the Shores. (The password for admittance is "Presto!") All donations should be sent to The Veterans of Viral Wars in Mr. Owens' name.

Rebecca Beaker, 27, of drowning. The latest wife of Dr. Kenneth Beaker was found, face down, in their home swimming pool. Officers found no sign of foul play. Dr. Beaker was not home at the time and is reportedly heartbroken and in seclusion in Las Vegas. A glitzy Mardi Gras—themed memorial is planned for late next week, so be sure to bring your beads!

Robert "Mack" McIntyre, 49, of blunt trauma to the head. The story of the "Psychotic Neighborhood Butcher" came to a tragic end when Mack's body was found in an alley behind The Sleep-ee Time Travel Motel in Burbank, CA. The former child psychologist turned troubled meat-seller had been in a legal dispute, but few details are known. A wake will be held at his store where patrons are encouraged to recall how verbally abusive he'd become.

Sleazy Bear, 12, even more dead from multiple bee stings. The father bear in the much-loved "Dead Bear Family" series has passed away again, this time from a run-in with a beehive. He is sorta survived by the rest of his dead bear family—Cheezy, Weezy, and Breezy. Honey donations can be made at their den. Word to the wise: drop off the honey at the door and run like hell.

Lt. Jerry Farner, 24, by Horde attack. Lt. Farner was on his second tour of duty as part of The Great Pushback when, for reasons unknown, he decided to hug a free-ranger. Not pretty. He was preceded in passing by his 4 brothers, 4 sisters, and 2 or 3 half-brothers in that trailer park on the east side of town. Oh yeah, and his half-sister that he hardly ever saw. Military ceremony to be held at the VVW building with a bland lunch afterwards.

Engagements

Dr. Kenneth Beaker, 47, to **Ms. Kandace Lipps**, 22, a dancer/entertainer at Pixie's Flesh Ranch in NV. Date to be announced.

Divorces

Sen. Frederick Meep, 52, and **Janice Shriver Meep**, 48, of irreconcilable differences.

Escapes

"Jiffy," age unknown, a former post-lifer who is believed to have gone Horde. Do *not* approach on your own; he is considered one-armed and dangerous. Should be easily distinguishable by his faded name tag. Contact the Paraguard (1-877-SLAMMER) if you know of his whereabouts. A stamp reward is offered.

THE ANSWERS!

WERD SURCH 1

Page 2

L-l-let's s-see h-h-how you d-did!

THE QSCALE EXPRESS!

Page 4

1. d; 2. d; 3. c; 4. c; 5. b; 6. c; 7. d; 8. d; 9. d; 10. c

CROZZWERDZ 1

Page 5

SHAPE UP!

Page 8

1. d.; 2. d.; 3. c.; 4. d.; 5. d.; 6.–8.: Your guess is as good as mine.

Judging your score:

1–2 correct: **Total tool**; 3–4 correct: **Maroon**; 5–6 correct: **Brilliant maroon**;

7–8 correct: **Very brilliant maroon, like one a them book types who use the purdy words.**

QuizzzTime!!!: SALLY'S BIG ADVENTURE

Page 15

1. False; 2. False; 3. False; 4. False; 5. False; 6. True; 7. True; 8. True

YOU COMPLETE ME!

Page 16

1. Ear ----> Pear, Tears, Fear, Dearest

2. Ate --->Mate, Grater, Plates, Threaten

3. Wan --->Swan, Wanes, Wanker, Wanted

4. Are ----> Mare, Rare, Share, Stares

5. And --->Hand, Bland, Sand, Grandé

THE DEADLY BLOCKS!

Page 20

```
      M O O

    R O O M
    M O O D
    L O O M
    M O O T

   M O O S E
   B R O O M
   G L O O M

  M O O N I E
  M A R O O N
  M O T I O N

 B L O O M E D
 C O N F O R M

Z O M B O T I C

A M O R P H O U S
```

BRAIN LABYRINTH

Page 24

QuizzzTime!!!: LOVE IN THE TIME OF P1V1

Page 34

1. True;   2. True;   3. True;   4. True;   5. True;   6. False;   7. True;   8. False

DR. KENNETH BEAKER, PhD, SCIENTIST, AND HUMANITARIAN WOULD HAVE A WORD WITH YOU...

Page 36

Femoral, Infection, Oblongata, Convulsions, Owwwww, Swollen, Pituitary, Mucus, Cranium, Ackkkkfff

DR. DOOFUS, ORGAN DETECTIVE!

Page 37

Heart, Kidney, Lungs, Tingler, Broccoflower Tumor

JAMBLE

Page 42

Roast

Broom

Stereo

Remove

Answer: "I Want a Torso, But Even More So!"

Houstallas, we have a—uhhhhh...

DOUBLE CROZZWERDZ!!

Page 47

```
P  I  A  Z  Z  A        D        Z
U                    P  I  Z  Z  A
Z        B              Z        T
Z        U        F     Z        O
B  L  I  Z  Z  A  R  D  Y        P
E        Z        A
                  Z
      G  R  I  Z  Z  L  E  D
         A     L           A
   L     Z     E           Z
F  R  I  Z  Z  Y     F  U  Z  Z  Y
      Z                    L
      Z        G  U  Z  Z  L  E  D
```

GOT A MATCH?

Page 48

Super pluggo, Laser hammer, Particle shears, Atom scrambler,
Molecular mitt, Vibro fork, Dimensional catapult, Robot lemurs

WERD SURCH 2

Page 49

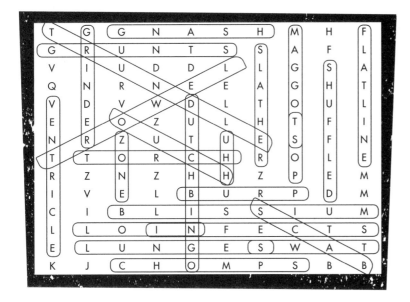

CRYPTIC CLUSTERFUN

Page 52

A. The Magna Carta; B. Vasectomy; C. Chico at the piano; D. A hula hoop;

E. Pat Robertson; F. Sundaez with Jiffy

THE TREMENDOUSLY BIG BONUS ANSWER: The Assassination of Archduke Ferdinand

PUT 'EM BACK TOGETHER, WILLYA?

Page 54

Drunks, Ladies, Dancer, Lifers, Whores, Police, Cosmos, Jaeger, Chomps, Lonely

QuizzzTime!!!: A ZOMBIE WALK FOR TIMMY

Page 58

1. True; 2. True; 3. True; 4. True; 5. True; 6. True; 7. True; 8. False

RHYMEZ WITH ?????

Page 59

1. Crunch; 2. Liver; 3. Skin; 4. Ribs; 5. Bleeds

TRIVI-UHH QUIZZZ!!

Page 62

Fo' sheezy!

1. Ear, Toe, Jaw, Rib, Lip, Gum. Bonus Answer: Noz.

2. Tempe, Provo, Sacracisco, Portlandia, Boise, Palinville.

3. Canada, Mexico, Japan, and China.

4. Ingesting any type of flesh or aerosol cheese.

5. Drug, Cable, Liquor, Garment, Food, Beauty, Tobacco, Dessert.

6. Two years or as long as you survive.

7. You poor thing—enduring questions *this* dumb.

8. Why, no—no, it doesn't.

9. Japan walled itself off after the P1V1 landed on its shores. Trick question—your friend Rob is full of shit.

10. Oh, come on—you had to look back *here*? Really? Dang.

WHERE THE H DID THE CONSONANTS GO???

Page 66

1. Sacracisco; 2. Houstallas/Ft. Worthstin; 3. Losandiego; 4. Pittsyldelphia;

5. Phoenixon; 6. Cleveland; 7. Orlanderdale; 8. Palinville;

9. Omaha/CouncilTucky; 10. Little Rocklahoma City

YOUR NUMBER'S UP!!

Page 76

1. 33; 2. 7; 3. 64; 4. 15; 5. 65; 6. My dead dog ate my homework; 7. See number 6; 8. Hike?

WERD SURCH 3

Page 77

B	A	W	B	W	P	A	I	N
R	O	W	I	E	U	K	Y	E
O	R	D	T	S	T	A	B	E
A	T	I	Y	C	R	O	A	K
C	A	R	O	T	I	D	Y	K
L	L	T	R	A	S	T	W	A
O	F	N	B	A	Y	H	V	P
T	E	A	G	E	S	U	U	U
S	V	P	W	E	T	D	W	N
C	E	J	O	E	M	A	O	P
R	R	T	N	K	M	P	U	U
E	Y	E	B	A	L	L	D	K
A	T	H	O	R	A	X	E	E
M	C	R	U	S	H	E	D	W

ZUDOKU!

Page 82

8	4	7
5	1	6
2	9	3

1	2	3
4	5	6
7	8	9

HANGDUDE!

Page 84

Puzzle #1: John Wilkes Kafka Booth

Puzzle #2: Horny, The Living Dead Unicorn

Puzzle #3: The Productiva Comedy/Variety Hour

CROZZWERDZ 2

Page 87

```
Z A R D O Z           S P A Z
    A                 C   M
  E C Z E M A         H A S
    E       G         I Z I T
Z   D   S O Y U Z     I   A
A D Z   Z   N     O N N
G       H   I L   G   Z
S C H N O Z Z A L     Z A
    I       E Z       Y
R A Z E D   S L E Z Y
```

THE EVEN DEADLIER BLOCKS!

Page 88

```
      T I E
    D I E T
    S I T E
    T I N E
    M I T E

  T I R E D
  I R A T E
  S T E I N
  T R I E D

  W R I T E R
  E D I T O R
  W A I T E D

S T E N C I L
S L E I G H T
F R I G H T E N
```

QuizzzTime!!!: CHOMPS GETS A ROOM

Page 94

1. False; 2. True; 3. True; 4. True; 5. True; 6. True; 7. False; 8. True

If you enjoyed *The Play & Werk Buk,* then look for these wonderfully derivative publications not coming from Sourcebooks in the near future!

Games That Suck: A Fang-Tastic Book of Puzzles and Such—

No matter what kind of vampire you are, you can't be fabulous and superhuman *all* the time. Even hot and pouty members of those "who walk the night" need to occasionally cut loose. If that sounds like you, then this is a book you can really sink your *teeth* into! Get it? *Teeth!*

NEW TRICKS FOR OLD DOGS: A MERRY MANUAL FOR WAYWARD WEREWOLVES—

How many canine-related gags can be worked in between two covers? I don't know, but you'll wear yourself out trying to count 'em all! It shouldn't take a silver bullet to make you understand what a howlin' good time you'll have when you get your paws on this pup. Roll over and fetch it, preferably before the full moon!

Gargantuan Lizard Serious Laff Party—

Japan's sensational humor/humiliation book finally makes its way to this country. Puzzles and jokes that only a gargantuan lizard could love. 4-D glasses included! (*Please note: this book has not been recalled.*)

Serial Killer Volume o' Joy—

Not all monsters are foreign and/or alien; some are just regular workin' class white guys. Give this jolly tome to your favorite serial killer and see if his gloomy mood doesn't brighten or, at a minimum, if he stops disappearing for days and/or smelling like bleach.

The Comedy Stylings of Zero and One—

This team of madcap robots is often referred to as "The Abbot and Costello of A.I.," and you'll understand why after reading this collection of their finest bits. Who can forget the classic "Who's on 011100001011100001?" *All* their timeless routines are here, translated into the crisp, clean realm of binary code. Warning: not to be ordered by humans. Give a copy to your tablet today!

Generic Monster Mayhem—

You say you don't fit into any of these trendy categories and you're simply a common freak? If that's the case, pay no mind to those other books, because *this* is one for you. Average games for ordinary creatures. So utterly normal, you'll feel like you almost fit in. Doesn't *that* sound different?

ABOUT THE AUTHOR

David P. Murphy, Ph.Z. (he obtained his Ph.Z. from the prestigious Port-Au-Prince Capon Academy), is a songwriter and producer of two CDs, *Shining in a Temporary Sun* and Henry Perry's *Effortless*.

He has been playing piano since he was a kid and is still trying to get it right.

After twenty-five years in Los Angeles, Mr. Murphy now resides in his hometown of Omaha, Nebraska, with his mutant orange tiger cat, Beany. He has recently completed his newest musical, *anotherwhere*, and will release a CD, *A Simpler Christmas*, with Camille Metoyer Moten in the fall of 2010. His next album, *Watching the Little Planes Land*, may finally find the light of day in 2011.

Zombies for Zombies: The Play and Werk Buk is his second buk. How many authors can say their second book has a "connect the dots" drawing? Huh?

For more information, please see www.davidpmurphy.com and www.zombiesforzombies.com.

ABOUT THE ILLUSTRATOR

Daniel Heard is an illustrator living in San Francisco.

He's drawn comic books such as *Phonogram* and *Comic Book Tattoo* for Image Comics, as well as illustrated several books (*The Mad Scientist Hall of Fame* and the *Z4Z* series). He wrote this in the third person and is available for work.

For additional info re: Daniel Heard, please see www.danielheard.squarespace.com.